LADIES, POWER UP YOUR BRAND

THE WOMEN ENTREPRENEUR'S GUIDE TO
GETTING PAID TO BE BOLD, BRILLIANT
AND UNAPOLOGETICALLY YOU

Faith James & Stacy Graiko

ISBN: 978-0-578-59703-4

This book is dedicated to women and girls everywhere, and especially, to Isabelle Grace, Madisyn and Brittany. Never lose sight of your power.

Table of Contents

Introduction 1

Prologue 7

SECTION I – On Brands and Branding 15

CHAPTER 1 – What is Branding and Why Does It Matter? 17

CHAPTER 2 – Personal Branding for Women is Unique 27

CHAPTER 3 – Lessons from the Power Women We Love 37

CHAPTER 4 – Unlocking Your Feminine Superpowers 45

SECTION II – Building Your Personal Brand 55

CHAPTER 5 – The Fundamentals: Discovering Your VPs 57

CHAPTER 6 – Your Brand Oath – The Power of
Authenticity 75

CHAPTER 7 – Aligning Brands: Your Ideal Client 81

CHAPTER 8 – Bring It Together: Your Power Brand
Blueprint 87

SECTION III – Rock Your Personal Brand 91

CHAPTER 9 – Power Mindset and Emotions 93

CHAPTER 10 – Power Presence – Dress the Way You
Want to be Addressed 99

CHAPTER 11 – Power Language 105

CHAPTER 12 – Get Focused: Do the Thing You Deeply
Love and Master It 113

Postscript: Money Moves 119

Women Everywhere: Let's See Your #PowerPose 123

Acknowledgements 125

Introduction

"She remembered who she was, and the game changed."
– Lalah Delia

The desire to be authentic is a human truth, and living authentically is a goal we all share. When we honor our authentic selves by living in a way that is aligned with who we truly are inside, we feel happier and more fulfilled. Our relationships with others are better, and we attract people to us. Our communication is clearer and we operate more effectively. As a business leader, this translates to higher profitability. Yet, many of us compromise our authenticity over the course of our lives and careers, for one reason or another. This book aims to help women get in touch with their authentic selves, through the process of personal branding.

There are many excellent books in the marketplace that help women get back in touch with themselves, reclaim their power, excel in leadership positions, and lead more fulfilling lives. Inspirational authors like Lalah Delia, Brene Brown, Barbara Stanny, Rachel Hollis, Sheryl Sandberg and many others have written exceptional books about women's empowerment and leadership.

We're thrilled that more women than ever are sharing their stories and helping other women become stronger. In general, women are making tremendous progress, becoming savvier, and assuming more leadership positions in business and government than ever before – partly because we are revealing our knowledge and experience through our personal stories and supporting each other on the way up.

But there is one vital element we have not found in any of the amazing books out there: clear instruction to help women step into their authentic selves through the process of brand-building, using the same approach employed by big, corporate brands. This is where we come in: our experience in advertising and marketing working with large, successful brands has provided us perspective about brand-building that has proven invaluable to our branding clients. We've developed a program exclusively for personal branding, aimed at women, and we've worked with hundreds of business leaders, entrepreneurs and political candidates throughout the past decade to help them uncover their true selves and live more authentically.

Starting with our work with The White House Project for women's leadership (where we trained alongside the likes of Marie Wilson and Gena Davis), and culminating in our current work at the Personal Branding Consultancy, we have had the pleasure of working with women from all different walks of life, learning about what holds them back, and what they need to move forward. We have been part of the growing movement in political leadership that is helping prepare more women than ever to run for public office, and we've helped women who have left corporate positions to start their own consulting, retail and service businesses.

Many of the women we've worked with have urged us to "write a book" to capture our program elements so that they can do it themselves, at their own pace; and also to put on record the more inspirational stories we've told to motivate them throughout the years. Those of you who have worked with us know that we are fond of sharing our own stories and regaling you with tales of corporate America – names are always changed to protect the innocent of course! – so we've included some of our favorite personal stories here, along with the nuts and bolts of the personal branding program we've developed.

Our book is part art, part science – accessible business know-how, based on experience and illustrated with personal stories. We call it *"Cosmo meets Harvard."* At its heart is everything we know and want to make known about personal branding that will help you get in touch with your authentic self, re-discover who you were meant to be, and use what you find to craft your career or business so you can reach your full potential. Personal branding is about unapologetically embracing who you are – no compromises.

We'll show you how to create your personal brand using the same disciplined approach to branding that we've taken with services, packaged goods, luxury and retail brands. And based on our experience as women working in the business world, we tailor this strategy to women leaders like you. You'll end up with a solid platform to continue building, and the knowledge to do so confidently.

How will having a strong brand benefit you as a business leader? There are many ways. Here are a few things we know to be true about strong brands:

- When your brand is clear, your ideal customers and clients find you.
- When your brand is different, your competition ceases to exist.
- When your brand is authentic, you feel supercharged at work and money flows to you with ease.
- When your brand delivers real value, you become irresistible and irreplaceable.

Yes, there is a certain amount of rigor required to develop and sustain your brand. When you do it right, branding isn't easy, but we can promise you it will be well worth the effort. Whether you're an entrepreneur, freelancer, side-hustler, or part of a team, we want to help you discover and build your personal brand the way the big brands do. Before we help you power up your brand, we must warn you about the phenomenon of #fake-branding (yes, it's so important we created a hashtag).

Much like "fake news," "fake branding" fails to deliver and leaves out crucial details. Unfortunately, there are plenty of branding knock offs out there, ready to take your money and build you a slick logo and lull you into believing you have built a powerful brand that will attract your ideal clients and help you achieve your goals. Well, here's a truth bomb: unless you're addressing both the psychological *and* tangible aspects of your brand, while utilizing a foundational blueprint approach, you are not building an authentic brand that will attract your ideal clients and create raving fans.

Now, we have a question for you: are you an "even though" and "nevertheless" kind of woman who confronts challenges head-on and moves through them without fear? If so, this book is for you. Through the information and exercises on the pages to follow, we aim to re-connect you with your authentic self, help you find more joy in your work, and achieve increased profitability in your business.

Throughout the following pages, we concentrate exclusively on branding, confident that once you understand the concept, you will understand the benefits of curating a powerful personal brand. We discuss the traps women often fall into when branding and promoting ourselves: the tendency to think we are not good enough; that someone else has already done what we want to do better than we ever could; and that we'll sound like a braggart when sharing our stories. We explore the causes of self-defeating attitudes, shatter the myths we tell ourselves; and share notable case studies of our successful women clients – all to guide you toward clarity in your purpose and greater effectiveness in your communications and relationships with your colleagues, clients, and customers.

If you're a woman who wants to remake or enhance your brand, this book is for you. If you're a woman who has never considered yourself a brand before and wants to develop your brand from start to finish, this book is for you. If you're a millennial embarking upon your career, a Gen X-er dealing with mid-life issues, or a woman who refuses to be labeled, this book is for you. Whether you're a business-owner whose personal brand and business brand is intertwined, or an employee of a company, this book is for you.

For maximum impact, we suggest that you read it from front to back, as our program is iterative and each section builds on the one before it. By the final chapter, you'll have created a solid foundation on which to build your brand and identified some areas to continue developing. We also invite you to join our Facebook group, The Savvy Branders Tribe, where you can interact with others and discover how they are building their brands, share your stories, get advice, and savor the exceptional company of other powered-up women.

We hope you enjoy the book. We look forward to connecting with you on social media and spending time together at one of our national or international branding events. Remember, we are all in this together.

Faith & Stacy

****

Prologue

You've either experienced them yourself, or know from observing others, the challenges women leaders face. We don't need to convince you that it's tough, and the struggle is real. However, here are some cold, hard facts about women's leadership to ground our conversation, help you understand why women need branding more than ever, and discover why we believe branding can benefit society as a whole.

Women are underrepresented in government, on corporate boards, and in leadership positions across all industries. IBM research shows that 79 percent of global companies haven't prioritized achieving gender equality in their workplaces. In the U.S., the Council of Foreign Relations ranks the United States as 20th in workplace equality. At this rate, the World Economic Forum has estimated it will take 202 years for the gender gap to close. In the US, just one percent of Fortune 500 CEOs are women and according to the 2019 Catalyst Women of the S&P 500 report, only 5 percent are women CEOs.

With efforts being made by terrific organizations to enact positive change, the trend is picking up slowly. As of 2017, more than 11.6 million firms in the US were owned by women, employing nearly 9 million people, and generating $1.7 trillion in sales. Still, women-owned firms (51% ownership or more) account for only 39% of all privately held firms and contribute 8% of employment and 4.2% of revenues (NAWBO 2017 research). This is clearly a problem, because the firms in which women are underrepresented are missing out on the unique skill sets that women hold. This effectively limits economic growth, keeps corporate cultures from taking advantage of balanced point of views, and frankly, seems a bit old-fashioned and short-sighted. The work we do is dedicated to closing the gap until women and men hold an equal share of leadership positions across categories. The world's population is gender balanced...why shouldn't our leadership be?

So why is it so important for women and men to lead equally?

To begin with, men and women bring different strengths to the table, due largely to our biology. Throughout the ages, men have fought enemies, kept their families safe, and hunted for food to survive. Women have birthed and nurtured offspring, fed their families, and soothed them when wounded. Men and women use complementary skill sets to accomplish these goals: men tend to be more pragmatic when solving problems, whereas women tend to be more intuitive (to break it down in simplistic terms, and yes there are a lot of nuances here). This results in an imbalance in teams when they are male- or- female dominated.

When a group of men work together in their pragmatic way, they may miss something that women may see, and vice versa. But when women and men *work together* and bring their unique problem-solving skill sets to the table, nuances are identified, energy is shifted, and ultimately, more is accomplished. When our needs and goals are represented, we add perspective that benefits more people, exponentially. Our collective goal as a society should be to create a balance that ensures leadership in all areas, benefits from the total skill set available from men and women working together. But with the numbers still stacked against true equality, we clearly have some catching up to do.

It's important to emphasize that in no way are we suggesting women act more like men in order to "fit in" to cultures that were created around male leadership styles. We are firmly in the camp that we *need to be who we are*: that women should not change to be more like men – but that we should encourage corporate cultures to adjust to the way women lead, so women and men may lead authentically, together. We also believe women have the power, and even an obligation, to help change these cultures, by asserting our true selves and using our loudest voices to be advocates for change.

Over the course of our careers, we have witnessed inequality in leadership firsthand. In general, women tend to be more reticent to speak up in meetings, preferring to communicate one-on-one, versus in a group. Often, we struggle to stand up for ourselves – and that includes not being willing to toot our own horn about our accomplishments, not speaking up when it's time to ask for a raise, choosing not to defend ourselves when necessary, and allowing mansplaining. As women, we too often lack the confidence to claim our seat at the table, or the desire to do so, knowing we bear responsibility for a multitude of other important things in our lives. Consequently, women tend to miss important opportunities to shine and are instead outshined by others. And sometimes, maddeningly, those who outshine us are *less* competent or *less* passionate about their ideas.

Can you relate?

And there is another even more alarming hot-button issue gaining visibility today in women's leadership circles: *women opting out* from leadership positions. Simply saying, "thanks, but no thanks" to climbing the corporate ladder, and making other choices for themselves and their careers. When this results in starting a business or joining with others to do so, we are all for it. In fact, that is probably the choice many of you reading this book have made – and we support you fully.

As well, lots of moms make the choice to stay home with the kids because this is the family's priority – thumbs up! This choice can be very powerful for those who are in the position economically and socially to make it.

But what we don't like to see is women opting out of the race altogether and deciding to forego their personal and professional goals because the corporate atmosphere is perceived as unaccommodating to women. If you are someone that has felt this, and considered leaving, take heart that you are not alone. This is something we can, and will, change with more women in leadership positions.

Remember, men have had many, many more years of practice honing their leadership skills, resulting in men generally feeling pretty confident at the head of the table – and this has created imbalances in power that women simply feel uncomfortable working around.

Structurally, many of the environments in which we work have been crafted over decades around men's needs and the ways they prefer to operate. Think about the top-down management structure that is slowly being replaced by webbed structures where responsibility is spread out more evenly across levels. The authoritarian lead-by-fear culture that was very present decades ago but is thankfully, slowly fading today. And, a complaint I hear often in my Facebook executive women's business travel group – the fact that you can't have dinner at the hotel bar without being subjected to unwanted conversation or sports on the TV monitors.

And then there are the logistics issues, like business travel, long commutes, expecting to be "on" 24/7 with greater connectivity – dealing with these things can get in the way of helping out in our kids' classrooms, attending our kids' games, and spending good quality time with those we love, and can further shake our desire to play the corporate game.

Finally, in a more subtle, yet pervasive and concerning way, are the hints built in to corporate settings that women are extraneous, an afterthought to teams that were built around men's needs and ways of working. We are talking here about pay inequality, sexual harassment, workload imbalance, and assumptions about qualifications, among other issues. Almost imperceptible cues that these issues are present can be damaging to team structures, reinforcing the perception that men are really the ones in charge.

To illustrate how corporate cultures can be less than ideal for women, here is one story that has stuck with us over the years: early on in one of our careers in advertising, after the 2000s - in a prestigious ad agency, a meeting was convened of our small team – myself, a female writer, a male art director and our VP group leader. We were a newly formed team focusing on interactive, web-based advertising, and were slowly building our business. Our manager, an old-school ad guy (think several cocktails over lunch and anytime boondoggle type) was trying to motivate us to produce more work, with the promise of success at the end of the rainbow. He told us, if we met our sales goals, there would be *"porsches and pussy for everyone!"* This he promised out loud, addressing us all, without any sense of embarrassment or awareness that we women may not actually be motivated by those things.

Just think about that: not long ago, this was acceptable behavior, language, and culture in corporate America. And I'm embarrassed to say that at the time we didn't think twice about what was said – he got no pushback, and nothing was ever reported to management. We women just exchanged glances and rolled our eyes, and then went on with our day.

It's good to know that today, thanks to more women present in corporate environments to censure bad behaviors, women can feel confident addressing this type of inappropriate conduct in the workplace. Though *how* it is dealt with, and the ultimate consequences, may still be less than ideal in some environments, telling us we still have some work to do.

The point is, the business culture was clearly set up around men's needs – and we need to change this to make the business culture more attractive for women. Our antidote to this is creating corporate cultures in which we can feel like ourselves, make contributions that count, and feel good about the work we do which takes up so much of our personal time.

We firmly believe that by acting together, we can change the status quo of the business culture and craft jobs, teams and cultures in a way that will appeal to women and inspire them to assume leadership positions across diverse industries.

If this resonates with you, this book is here to help! We assert that every woman has leadership abilities within her. Need proof? Just look at the busy mothers you know who manage to get their kids up, dressed, and where they need to go each day. Moms are famous for multi-tasking, and hell hath no fury like a mom challenged to attend a school event and ace a big presentation at work on the same day. Mom or not, women by our nature, have within ourselves innate abilities to rise to the occasion when needed. Harnessing this divine female energy is the secret to getting more women into leadership positions in business, public service, and politics.

"Be Better not Bitter!"

Throughout our experience in business we have seen women really shine: in the meeting where the female executive stands tall, captures the room's attention, and dazzles the audience with steak *and* sizzle. We have witnessed cooperative working partnerships consisting of women and men at the highest levels, where groups exceeded their original goals and objectives. It's these magical moments that have inspired us to really understand what's happening and try to recreate the factors leading to this type of collaborative success.

Usually in these situations we've observed several factors at play: a phenomenal culture, a balanced team, and an atmosphere that encourages opinions. This combination of factors is optimal, and paves the way for women to feel like they can be themselves.

But we have also seen these amazing peak events happen in less-than- optimal situations as well, driven by a woman's resolve to be the voice for change, action, and inspiration - as only a woman can be. In our experience, a woman that possesses unwavering conviction in her beliefs, accompanied by the self-confidence that comes from truly knowing herself, is a force to be reckoned with.

And this is the big audacious premise of this book and our work: that by knowing yourself intimately, you can release your superpowers and let your inner self shine with unbridled confidence to claim your seat at the table - whether that table is in business, politics, education or elsewhere. Our mission is to help women see themselves authentically, and in doing so, even the playing field across categories and industries, ages and locations. Now is our time...now is *your* time to shine.

On Brands and Branding

"All of us need to understand the importance of branding. We are CEOs of our own companies: Me Inc. To be in business today, our most important job is to be head marketer for the brand called You."

— Tom Peters

"Personal Branding is not about being famous. It's about being selectively famous."
— William Arruda, Personal Branding Guru

* * * * *

Making your own choices is what being a powerful brand is all about. Once you have a strong, robust brand, you make your own rules for yourself, attract your ideal clients, and achieve greater success.

But a book on branding isn't complete without a lesson in the fundamentals: what is a brand, anyway? How is branding a woman different from branding shoes? What are some women brands you can draw inspiration from? The following chapters will set the stage for you to gain a deeper understanding of the ideas and theory behind branding, so you can understand it at its core - and then we can move ahead to the important business of building yours.

Full speed ahead! Let's dive in.

♥

CHAPTER 1

What is Branding and Why Does It Matter?

"Any fool can put on a deal, but it takes genius,
faith and perseverance to create a brand."
– David Ogilvy

There are many, many definitions of "brand," but our favorite is, a "unique promise of value." Simply put, a brand is an authentic, one-of-a-kind offering to the world. It is *not* a logo, a tagline, or a visual alone – although they are all expressions of a brand. However, a brand encompasses so much more: it is intangible and tangible, unseen and seen. It represents truth and aspiration, virtues that connect the brand with its customers over the long term. Built on vision, purpose, values, and passions, it exudes a specific tone of voice and presents a distinctive look and feel in the channels that link it to its customers and potential customers.

Strong brands follow the 3 Cs of branding: clarity, consistency, and constancy. They are *clear* about who they are and what they stand for; they *consistently* show up in the same way, staying true to who they are and what they stand for; and they *constantly* talk to their customers and potential customers to remain foremost in their minds.

The key to a company's financial success lies in the strength of its brand. Each year, WPP produces BrandZ – a high-profile list of the world's most valuable brands. The ranking considers many factors, including financial performance, but notably looks at how consumers perceive and feel about brands, placing high value on the strength of the brand in the mind of the consumer – in other words, the perception the brand has created.

In 2019, Amazon, Apple, and Google, top the list of most valuable brands – correlating how their brands are perceived by consumers, with their financial worth. The takeaway? The stronger your brand, the more profitable your business. This explains why there is so much emphasis on branding in the corporate world.

So, how does a brand operate?

A brand puts a distinct, unique idea into the minds of consumers, enabling them to decide quickly and easily if that brand is for them. Have you ever said or heard someone say, "I'm a [Brand X] person?" That's because brands make a concerted effort to promote a unique identity that will enable its target customers to choose them. Through powerful, emotional connective strategies implemented over time, they cement an image of themselves in the public consciousness, helping consumers discover and understand the brand's purpose and value for themselves, even if they have not personally used it. This strategy of offering consumers shortcuts to understanding – known in the industry as heuristics – allows them to choose the brands that speak to them and reject the brands that don't. An entrepreneur, business, or company that targets its brand effectively can expect immediate sales, long-term loyalty, and repeat sales, which results in...you guessed it: profits!

To illustrate the point, consider two rival automotive brands: Chevrolet and Ford. Chances are, even if you've never owned one of these vehicle brands, your mind quickly leapt to a preference for one or the other. You may not be able to explain why that happened; it could have been something you read, saw or heard from the brands themselves that led to you to align yourself with one over the other.

Try it again for some other brand categories: are you a Coke or Pepsi person? Macy's or Kohl's? Nike or Adidas? Over time, these companies have crafted their brands so effectively that your reaction to them is second nature. If you start to really examine your brand loyalties, and the choices you've made about brands, you'll soon understand the power of developing a brand for yourself.

There is a science to building a brand, with key components to it.

Make no mistake, great brands aren't merely wished into existence – they are built, with key, common building blocks. Among these: the founder's passion and vision; the products or services it can reasonably and credibly offer and deliver well given its resources (e.g. intellectual capital, people and money); and its target customers' wants, needs, and willingness to buy – in other words, the marketplace. When building your brand, you must consider all these factors because if your brand does not align with them, it will not be authentic…and will ultimately fail.

The "unique promise of value" principle works for all brands, whether big or small, hard goods or services, corporate or personal. We'll soon get into personal brands, but first let's take a deeper look at some big corporate brands to understand the basics of how they are using branding.

When you think about the largest, most well-known brands, you can probably easily conjure an image in your mind along with some unique feelings with it. Consider Apple. For most people, the Apple brand evokes images and feelings in the territory of sleek, smart, clean, and creative. You might also think expensive, snobby or exclusive. How about Disney? Many people immediately think of family, fun, and characters. You might also think expensive, hot and crowded.

Why are the images and feelings you associate with certain brands consistent with other consumers? Because these brands have invested billions of dollars in crafting the stories and emotions they want people to experience when they think of their brands. This includes communications like advertising and marketing, as well as the experiences they offer with their products.

For Apple, think of the experience you have using your iPhone, iPod or Mac, and for Disney, experiences you've had or heard about with the parks, movies and TV shows. It's important to note these associations can be a result of your personal experience or word of mouth – and increasingly, because of social media's reach, brand perceptions are formed and promoted largely online. It is entirely possible to form an expectation about a brand without ever having actually experienced it for yourself. Think about that as you consider what people you have never even met may think about your brand. You need a strategy to make sure they think of you accurately, and don't form their opinions based on what others may think.

Apple and Disney have built their brands on their unique promise of value - the things they could offer that no one else could - and they continue to promote what makes them unique to ensure they stay relevant to their ideal customers. When you think about IBM PCs, do the adjectives sleek, smart, clean and creative come to mind? Probably not – at least not in the same way they do for Apple. And although families looking for fun can find a myriad of entertainment options available, none of them compare to the depth and credibility of Disney characters. Both Apple and Disney started with introspection: they looked inward to determine what they could deliver to consumers -- while remaining true to their mission – and then extended their message outward. As a personal or small business brand, you can do the same.

A brand provides a guiding light that attracts your customers and potential customers to you. In clear terms, it tells them that if they need what you are selling, you are the best and only option for them. For you, it clarifies your value and keeps you focused on the services and products you can deliver in the most unique way.

Imagine Apple or Disney trying to sell products that are way outside of what they are known for. Brands falter when they try to do too much and be too many things to their customers. A jack-of-all-trades is not consistent with a strong brand. To be a strong brand, you must have focus. While it's okay to "major" in one area and "minor" in another, the areas must relate to each other authentically, and both must connect back to your unique promise of value to your customers and potential customers.

Let's take Disney as an example again. Let's *pretend* (because this has not happened) they want to capitalize on the strength of their brand and its connection to parents by opening a chain of wine shops. Disney would have to ensure these stores aligned with their unique promise of value – offering fun, family-focused experiences, with character themes. Can you picture this? Chardonnay merchandised in a castle display...Belle and the Beast drinking Pinot Noir from Chip...?

Now think about a consumer who is shopping for relaxing adult beverages after a long hard day of work. Is this the type of store that would appeal to them? Probably, almost certainly, not. So, we can screen this idea out for Disney, simply because we know about its brand and the values, character and perceptions it carries.

One of the benefits of a strong brand is that it gives the brand owner a filter through which to look at potential new products and services, and decide what is right and what is not. Though it requires effort to build a brand, in the long run having a brand actually makes operating your business and connecting with your customers easier.

The good news for personal brands is they can employ the same principles, but act more nimbly and be more experimental than big brands like Apple and Disney.

So let's get a little closer to home now and talk about your personal brand. Your brand is mighty: it empowers you to support the people you are here to serve; it illuminates your path and purpose; and helps you achieve your goals, whatever they may be. We call this a "power brand" (or "pow-her" brand if we're being bold) - because you can move faster than big brands. You can be stealthy when stealth is needed, and nimble when nimbleness is required. You can turn the ship on a dime to avoid collisions or move toward opportunities, and you can power up all areas of your life - not just your business – using your brand. Think of personal branding as your power play.

This is why we always say that as a person, adopting branding principles and behaving like a brand is perhaps the most significant thing you can do for your business.

In addition to being able to move fast, another strong advantage personal brands have over corporate brands is that they have an actual personality that can be leveraged. When you are working on developing or refining your brand, think about yourself as a whole person, not just the *you* at work, or the *you* with your family. Incorporate all the richness of your life's experiences into your personal brand. You'll want to integrate all aspects of yourself into your professional brand for *maximum authenticity, which will* translate to both business success and personal fulfillment.

And remember - your brand will not only serve a marketing function for you professionally, but it will also be a guiding light for the way you think about and design your life's goals, your relationships with your family and friends, and most importantly, your relationship with yourself. It can help you vet people, experiences and money decisions, so that all are working in the service of your brand – Brand You, #youareyourbrand.

But why should you go through all this trouble? The reality is that people are going to judge you, no matter what. It's up to you to explain who you are, what you are about, and what you can offer. If you don't, they'll fill in the blanks for you - and sometimes, they won't get you right. How many times have you felt like you were unfairly labeled by a client, or passed over for a job you would be great at, or - the worst! - somebody else said something you've always thought and got tons of credit for it? If any of these things have happened to you, you need to ask yourself why. What is holding you back from telling the world what you really stand for, informing potential clients what you can do for them, or assuring future clients how you can serve them? The answer is a) lack of clarity, b) lack of confidence, or c) both. The solution? **Craft your brand story to tell others what you are all about.** *Tell them, before they tell your story for you.*

Small business have some unique considerations.

We get it: in the beginning, you take on every client who hires you, just to build your business. You act like a chameleon, stretching yourself to accommodate whatever said client wants, just to get the project. You may offer one specialty to one client, and pitch yourself as having another to the next. You jump at every prospect, because you're afraid if you don't, you'll have no business. But this can quickly put a business out of business, because clients get confused when they don't know what to expect. As we are fond of saying to our new small business clients – *You must stand for something, or you'll fall for anything.*

Once you gain clarity about your brand, you can be more selective about the clients with whom you enter into a contract for services. Once you have powered up your brand, you'll attract more clients that align with your values and what you have to offer. Then, to borrow a phrase from a popular insurance commercial, you can shift into "she shed" mode -- shedding the clients who no longer serve your brand.

Once you have developed a brand platform that feels authentic to you and helps you attract and serve your ideal clients, it's time to grow. For smaller brands, growth can be difficult. Due to the lack of shareholders (who drive expectations for large brands), smaller brands have different goals. As a solo-preneur or a small business-owner with a few employees, you may be tempted to celebrate when you have money left over for marketing after you pay your employees' salaries. But here's a reality check: to maintain a strong business, you must think beyond this month's revenue.

Our dear friend and client Diana Miret, the Business Profit Coach, often tells the story of a small leather goods brand from whom she'd bought a purse. A few months later, the owner personally followed up with her to see how she was enjoying her purse and to ask if she had any questions. This small, but significant step led her to make a subsequent purchase and strengthened her loyalty to the brand. Diana's story underscores the fact that as a small business, you must think about *attracting new* customers while *delighting existing* customers at the same time.

This is a key point of difference between big and small brands: data shows that small brands grow by attracting business away from competitors, whereas big brands achieve growth by selling more to their existing customers (Kantar, Mastering Momentum report, 2019). As a small brand, you only have so many products to sell, and you cannot constantly create new products like the big brands can. Sure, you can and should innovate and develop product extensions -- like an online course or a book -- in addition to your consulting services - but unlike a big brand, you likely can't acquire a new company to meet your customers' latest needs. Additionally, your smaller clients have limited resources and will deplete their budgets at a certain level. And even though they love you, they simply cannot buy more from you.

So, you've got to focus on acquiring *more* customers – and these customers will most likely come from your competition. To lure these customers away from your competitors, you've got two important tools in your toolkit: your brand and your size -- both of which are assets when used strategically.

Now let's get onto the business of discovering and building your unique power brand.

IT'S TIME TO POWER UP...

Start the process by obtaining a brand journal. And we're not talking about a piece of paper or a random notebook. Buy a beautiful journal you really enjoy and dedicate it to your brand development. You are going to write, by hand (!) – in this journal. There are a few (scientific) reasons for writing by hand:

- Handwriting your thoughts versus typing them will make you more selective with your words. You'll have to consider them more carefully – and we really want considered thoughts to form the basis for your brand.

- Handwriting versus typing something cements that thing in your memory, so you'll be able to recall it when needed. This is important when creating brand assets you'll want to be able to articulate easily later.

- Handwriting is not something you're probably used to doing every day, so the simple act of changing your process can stimulate the brain to think about things differently. This will create new perspectives for your brand.

Once you have your journal, at the top of the first page, write the following affirmation:

I am my brand and my brand is powerful.
I am my brand and my brand is powerful.
I am my brand and my brand is powerful.
I am my brand and my brand is powerful.

Fill the entire page with this affirmation. *Why*, you ask? Because repetition is the first law of success. You are about to embark on a powerful journey, and your mindset is the first and most important thing we want to influence. You must begin with the conviction that this is *your* time and *your* moment to shine. If you don't believe it, no one else will. To achieve it, you must believe it. As we can attest from our own experience, repetitive writing of your affirmations is a critical first step in the power-up branding process. We employed this practice to build our own brands and platforms, and we've been doing it ever since.

So, write on:

I am my brand, and my brand is powerful!

****

CHAPTER 2

Personal Branding for Women is Unique

> "We need women who are so strong they can be
> gentle, so educated they can be humble, so fierce
> they can be compassionate, so passionate they can
> be rational, and so disciplined they can be free."
> – Kavita Ramdas

> "Stop being apologetic. Take the power chair with
> ease and grace."
>
> – Faith & Stacy

When we approach the topic of branding with women, we often at first get pushback: for many women, just thinking about building a personal brand poses significant challenges and seems to fly in the face of femininity. Some things we've heard women say about thinking of themselves like a brand:

- I'll have to be inauthentic and not act like myself

- I don't have anything novel to say! How can I build a whole brand platform around *nothing*?

- Focusing on myself will take my focus away from others and will waste valuable time

Does any of this sound familiar?

But here's the good news: none of these assumptions is accurate. Discovering your brand is all about reconnecting with who you truly are, and being true to your nature. That means you don't have to act in a way that makes you uncomfortable, makes stuff up, or give up the important people and connections in your life. Being a brand aligns with your most cherished desires, goals, and priorities. Rather than distracting from what's important to you, it can actually help you achieve want you want.

When we share this alternative way of thinking about a personal brand with the women we work with, it gives them license to feel more confident – and inspired -- about creating their brands. So take heart: if your first instinct tells you to reject the idea of branding, rest assured, you're not alone. By re-framing the topic, we aim to help you feel energized and invigorated about creating a personal brand and enjoying its many benefits. In the following chapters we'll show you how to build your authentic brand, but first let's take a look at some of the barriers that can hold women back from fully embracing developing their personal brands.

We'll address these barriers one at a time, and show you how we think about brands.

Barrier #1: If I build a brand, it will be fake, and everyone will see through it

Ah, the dreaded "imposter syndrome" – something to which many of us can relate. This is a legitimate concern: being inauthentic – *a fraud* - could be catastrophic to you, your relationships, and your leadership position. However, you can breathe a deep sigh of relief because that is not what branding intends to do. Being a brand is about having a great awareness of who you are, what you can offer to others, and the way you show up in service to them – quite the opposite of what many people think. As you saw in the previous chapter, big corporate brands don't just *make it up*; they build their brands based on what is true to them and important to their people. When these two things match, you find your ideal customers.

We've said it before, but it bears repeating: we won't allow you to make things up and fabricate a personality that doesn't exist. You'll hear us talk about authenticity a lot. We believe nothing is more important to creating fulfilling personal and professional lives, and creating powerful connections with others, as being your authentic self is.

The exercises in this book demand truth, introspection, and honesty. Once you have developed your brand, it will feel so real, true, and authentic that you will want to shout it from the rooftops...not in an obnoxious way but with an aura of confidence that announces to the world, "Here's who I am and what I believe in." Again, release all doubt and worry about the process of building a brand. We guarantee, the end result will NOT be fake; it will be as real as the work you put into it, and at the end, you'll feel like the best version of yourself, just like one of the women we work with, who put it this way: *"I knew who I was before, but going through the process of looking at myself as a brand just brought the real me out even more. Now I feel like me, times 1000."*

How do you go about finding what is true for you? It starts with your building blocks: your character, your talents, and your hopes and dreams for the future. In the following chapters, we'll take you through the VPs of every strong brand: vision, purpose, values and passions. These qualities are unique to each one of us. If we asked 100 women for their VPs, we would receive 100 sets of unique answers. When you do these exercises, we want you to think long and hard about them to ensure your building blocks are robust. If not, your brand will not feel right. On the contrary; your brand's inauthenticity will make you feel terrible. Sooner or later, the chinks in your armor will show, and you will miss out on all the fabulous things that happen when you have a strong brand. You can begin thinking about these building blocks now -- even if only in the back of your mind – so you can tackle them head on when the time comes.

What happens when a brand operates on false VPs? Here is an example to bring this to life - one not based on any specific woman, but a combination of several women we've known. Imagine a CPA who excels at her job but feels most like herself in a casual environment. She has many corporate clients and she plays the part she thinks she should when she visits them, wearing suits and pantyhose and high heels. She feels like a fraud, but she does it anyway. One day, a client unexpectedly stops by her office to find her in her casual glory: jeans, sweater, tennies. She's a bit taken aback by the surprise visit and forgets she's not in her "corporate attire" – she's simply feeling like her authentic self, and they go on to have a passionate, productive conversation about her client's finances. Days later, the client sends her a note telling her how much she enjoyed their chat, and our friend starts reflecting on what went right. Note: this is a key component to learning about yourself and your brand – not only looking at what goes *wrong* when it does, but what goes *right*, and why.

In looking back at the conversation, our girl remembers she felt a lot like herself...more so than she normally would in talking to the client - and she remembered that she was in her own, comfortable environment, and she was wearing her comfy clothes in which she felt like her true self.

Granted, this example is based on a woman's choice of attire, which is only one (some would say small) part of your brand. But with your personal brand, everything counts. How you look, what you wear and how you present yourself are all vital elements of your brand that can signal authenticity - or inauthenticity - to you and everyone else.

Similarly, had she compromised a value, like integrity, or pretended to have a passion for something she actually does not like simply to connect with a client (do we really care *that* much about sports?) - her inauthenticity may have created a disconnect that could also be detrimental to her brand.

You must be true to who you are always, or you won't succeed. An effective way to gauge whether you're doing something inauthentic is to listen to your intuition. If it feels right, it probably is -- and if it doesn't, you must re-think your plan with authenticity at its very core.

Barrier #2: I don't know if I truly have anything new to say

In our experience, much of the hesitation about building a brand stems from this myth. Many of us simply don't think we have what it takes to be a brand: we don't have enough important things to say, so why go to the trouble of crafting a way to say it? Or, we have nothing new to add to the conversation. Or, we think other people – experts, authors, competitors – already say it much better than we ever could. Such negative thoughts contribute to the erroneous perception that we don't deserve a seat at the table. The result? We make no effort to get there. Ladies, this is brand suicide! If you can relate to this way of thinking, you *have got to* tackle this mindset first. Challenging any deeply ingrained negative beliefs about yourself and your capabilities is the first step to building your brand.

Here's the truth: there are only so many ideas. However, if an idea has never been done by *you* before, it's IS unique. Each one of us has a distinctive and valuable perspective on virtually every topic; therefore, we all have something of value to add.

Within your business, job, or leadership role, you have unique contributions to make. You're going express your idea differently, draw a unique picture of it, or tell a different story about it- something about *your* idea will be different, and your unique spin on it will be worthy of consideration by others. Your unique spin has the power to change someone's opinion, perceptions, and even their life. And guess what? Your unique spin is your *legacy*. It is what you will be remembered for, and what people will write about in your obituary someday far in the future. It's what your children will recall when asked about their mom and what she was like.

Think about this: what do you want to be remembered for? What is your unique addition to the world we live in? Sure, the ideas are out there and countless people are working on them - but your unique contribution can further the effort and add a perspective that just might shift the conversation in an unexpected way. For the sake of your legacy, let's pursue this further.

We challenge you to work through an idea you've had floating around your head - whether it's still in its infancy and needs a push from you to come to fruition, or it's a full blown idea you've been thinking about for years. Today, identify your unique contribution to the concept: it could be a fresh way of looking at it, a new way to talk about it, a unique anecdote to share about the topic - put a flourish on your idea and punctuate it uniquely so there is no mistaking it for someone else's baby. Then, re-look at it, and see if the old belief that you don't deserve a seat at the table still holds. We've done this exercise dozens of times with women in all kinds of industries, and we find it to be very effective. Chances are after you do it, you'll be feeling more confident that you *do* have something of value to offer the world.

Barrier #3: It's selfish to focus on myself

Can you relate to this? Women devote so much of their time attending to the needs of everyone around them, they often neglect their own basic needs – not to mention their bigger life goals. You know what I mean: your spouse is going through a mid-life crisis, your daughter is coping with challenges at school, and your parents are dealing with health insurance issues. Everyone needs *your* help. Why do we ride to the rescue? Because we're competent. Because if we don't do it, it probably won't get done right. Because we love them and we want to use our extraordinary talents to help others. Yet in our willingness and enthusiasm for solving other's problems, we sometimes (often?) sacrifice our own needs. We forget to assess the amount of time and energy we give to everyone else, versus ourselves. We fail to place a value on our time since it doesn't even occur to us.

And all tasks are not equal; some fit into our lifestyle without detracting from time spent with loved ones, while others require our total commitment and willingness to sacrifice quality time. We need to consider how much each task requires, and what it's worth to us - and reject the old feminine programming that all tasks require equal time. If we don't, we'll drive ourselves crazy trying to fit it all in, and wondering why we aren't really getting anywhere. Corporations assign value to each task, based on the worthiness of each task. If we want to achieve our goals, it's imperative that we repel the time wasters and embrace efforts that will move us closer to our true selves.

One way to do this is to believe in and adopt an approach of servant-leadership. Servant-leadership says that you lead others by serving them, but as a leader you must be judicious about how you spend your time, because your time is theirs, as much as it is your own. You know the adage about putting on your own mask on an airplane first? We help others best when we ourselves are feeling strong. As our client Doris Eggens, CEO of Live Well, Be Well likes to say, *your health is your wealth*. Put self-care at the top of your to-do list.

POWER UP...

_____

Now, grab your journal.

Affirm the following right now by committing it to paper:

> *I deserve a seat at the table.*
> *I have something unique to add to the world.*
> *The world is better off because I am in it.*
> *Taking care of me is taking care of others*

Exercise #1

Now let's tackle that myth that you have nothing unique to say.

Dedicate the next few pages to capturing your idea for a business, a business strategy, a speech, a book, a screenplay, etc. – anything you've been considering for a long time, but have been unable to action for whatever reason. Write next to it how it will be unique coming from you. Then, add a few more elements that will make it unique – and keep going until you can't think of any more.

Then read it through. Ask yourself, could this come from someone else? Your colleague, your competitor? If the answer is yes, add more details that makes it uniquely yours. Is there a story you are known to tell that can add unique details to your idea? An experience you had that can make the idea ownable only by you? Verbiage, a way of speaking, signature saying, drawings... Add anything that puts your unique stamp on the idea.

Don't worry about how messy this gets: you are allowed to cross things out, circle, star, underline – and start fresh on the next page. In journaling, messiness can be helpful. You'll sort things out this way. You are creating something wonderful: eventually your genius will shine through the chaos.

Give yourself permission to take, as we call it, "massive imperfect action." Your idea doesn't have to be perfect, it just has to be *"good enough"*. You can sort out the details later – but if you wait for perfection, you'll lose valuable time.

It's also helpful to think about this exercise as a purge, getting as many ideas as you have onto paper. Full-fledged ideas, half-formed thoughts, nuggets – any idea you have that could possibly, potentially, hopefully someday turn into something satisfying for you. Write it down!

You'll edit later, once you graduate from the journal and are ready to start putting your brand plan into a presentation format.

For now, just brain dump.

Write, right now. Edit nothing!

Exercise #2:

Let's start thinking about that legacy you'll leave – which later will form the building blocks for your purpose. What do you want to leave behind when you're gone? Your handbag collection, jewelry, real estate and money are great, but what do you want to be remembered for?

An exercise we find helpful is writing your own obituary. Don't panic: you're going to think well ahead, many, many years into the future. What is it you hope your kids and grandkids and friends and colleagues will say about you?

That you had great ideas but didn't action them? That you settled for good enough always, and never strived for great? That you had knowledge and talent to help others but chose not to?

These are probably not the headlines you want coming out at your funeral.

So write what you would want them to say. What lights you up, when envisioning what people will say about you someday? What would you be most proud to hear about yourself? That you took chances, risked failure, helped others. You built something tangible, you affected others positively, you bettered the world somehow. Take some time to write a detailed obituary for your local – or even the national or global - press. This will help you gain clarity on where you should take your brand next.

CHAPTER 3

Lessons from the Power Women We Love

"A strong woman is one who feels deeply and loves fiercely. Her tears flow as abundantly as her laughter. A strong woman is both soft and powerful, she is both practical and spiritual. A strong woman in her essence is a gift to the world." – Native American saying

"You must stop letting irrelevant sh*t hold you back. Forget what you think you can't do, and focus on what you want to do. Put yourself out there and you'll find your success."
– Faith & Stacy

To get you powered-up as you think about your own personal brand, let's look to some female brands we know and love - an excellent resource for finding inspiration to build your brand. Powerhouse women have the budget and scope to do brand-building right, with the most effective tools at their fingertips. They've built, tried, tested, and refined their brands to the ideal. You can employ their best practices for your own brand. Let's examine what these women are doing well, with exceptional results, and find some inspiration in these ladies.

When you think about women power brands, Oprah often comes to mind. She built her dynasty by following her intuition and doing what felt authentic to her - even when others told her she was crazy. One of our favorite Oprah stories is about her days as a junior anchor at a local station when she discovered that the women were paid much less than the men. She vowed to fix this disparity but had to leave the network and start her own company to do it. Even as a young professional, Oprah had the conviction to stand up for what she believed in. You might say she was clear on her brand. She followed her authenticity – and look where it got her.

Alexandria Ocasio-Cortez (AOC) is another example of a power brand. AOC believes in her principles so strongly she goes to the mat for them every time. Sure, she cares what people think of her - but to her, other people's opinions about her *ideas* matter more than what they think of her personally – and she makes this clear time and time again. If she comes across as pushy or aggressive, she leans into it, secure in the knowledge that she is fighting for the right things. She is committed to her convictions and to acting authentically at all costs.

What are some branding principles Oprah and AOC share? To begin with, clarity: they know who they are, and they stand firm in their truths. Confidence – borne of the strength of their convictions - is another quality they both have. When the going gets rough, and it has, for both of them, they maintain the confidence to stay the course.

These two power-women also possess grit, as evidenced by their work ethic and absolute commitment to their missions. Grit is the perseverance and conviction to keep going toward your goals, no matter how hard it gets. It's in the face of adversity where we are really tested – and these two ace the test time and time again. Success did not come easy to either one: Oprah spent many years slogging away in media, while AOC worked 18-hour shifts as a waitress and bartender before running for Congress. Through it all, their purpose and vision have guided their way. Both these women bring their authentic selves to the work they do every day, and their brands communicate who they are extremely clearly.

Now let's contrast Oprah and AOC to women you may recognize who are *not* powerhouse brands - but might like to be. We have a friend we'll call Carrie, who runs a very successful art business in Chicago. Carrie is the total package: talented, professionally savvy, and outgoing. When you see her artwork, you just know you want to own some of it because her designs – which are far and above anything you can buy in mass retail – ooze mid-century cool. People pay top dollar for her creations, and she's been featured in art and design blogs and magazines. Carrie's studio is in the Chicago Arts District, and she travels from art show to art show selling her pieces, interacting with wholesalers and attending art openings. On top of that, she and her successful consultant-boyfriend take frequent vacations to South America, Mexico and Europe.

When in the process of expanding her business to the east coast, Carrie was invited to do a pop-up shop at a fellow artist's studio on the seacoast near Boston, in a high-end arts area. She planned to fly out from Chicago to Boston, do the show, meet some contacts, and fly home. We had just started working with her, so when she told us about her plan, we felt pure excitement and exhilaration for her and the opportunities unfolding for her business. Mostly, we wanted to celebrate her success, but we were surprised by what we heard when we offered our congratulations. *"Yeah,"* she replied - *"it's almost like I have a bona fide business and I'm taking a legitimate business trip to sell real products."*

Let's pause to let that sink in. Her first instinct was to downplay her success, *not* join us in celebrating it. Does this sound familiar? Many women respond this way because they don't want to seem braggadocios, offend other people, or make them feel badly about their own success, or lack thereof. It's inherent in our feminine nature to automatically deflect praise, detracting from our own successes -- often to our own detriment.

What is often happening is we are actually questioning ourselves – and we do this regardless of the level of success we have achieved. In our minds, it's never enough success, money, or achievement. We should have accomplished more by now. Surely, somebody made a mistake and doesn't know we're not the real deal. We should have worked harder and been better. We "should" all over ourselves…and take away our own power in the process.

What is the net effect of this mindset? By telling ourselves we aren't good enough we start to act like we aren't. Sooner or later this becomes a self-fulfilling prophecy where we don't measure up anywhere. I recently saw a Facebook post that underscores this point. It read: *"Be careful what you say to yourself, your cells are listening!"* That simple statement contains an eternal truth, one with which we are familiar. We've all heard of the concept, "you become what you think", yet despite countless references to this fact, we as women are either unable or unwilling to heed the warning, preferring instead to suffer along and continually chastise ourselves.

Let's examine another scenario you may relate to. You spend weeks searching for the perfect outfit for your child's birthday party. When the day finally arrives, you get dressed, do your hair, and apply your makeup expertly. At the party, you celebrate your son with joy and confidence, feeling on top of the world thanks to all of your preparation and the smart choices you've made. Then, one of your mom-friends approaches you to tell you how wonderful you look. How do you respond? Rather than say, "Thanks, I love the outfit I put together too; it took me weeks to find just the right pieces," you act surprised and ex-claim, "*Oh really? Thanks, I got it on sale at TJ Maxx....*" totally downplaying the role *you* had in making it fabulous. In turn, the mood of the conversation shifts from elated to conciliatory: a seemingly small but impactful shift that detracts from what could have been a peak moment.

This is what women DO! We find it supremely difficult to claim our role in our success and take credit for our efforts. It is one of the key factors preventing us from achieving our desired goals. Why? And what can we do about it?

When we sat down with Carrie to help her develop more con-fidence, we learned she had been successful despite herself: she had no real sense of her brand, and her business plan was shal-low at best. Because she lacked definition and clarity about who she was and what she wanted to achieve with her business, she simply could not pinpoint any successes. Carrie needed brand milestones to assess whether what she was doing was on track with what she truly wanted for her business. Together, we worked on the fundamentals of her brand: her vision, purpose, values and passions. We envisioned the life she wanted to be liv-ing and created a roadmap to get her there.

Immediately after doing the exercises, Carrie started to see herself differently. Once she realized that she was, in fact, doing what she felt truly passionate about, and that her ideal life was within reach, she felt much more confident in her success. Within a couple of months, she started to see real progress toward her life's goals and began to walk taller and prouder. The key to get-ting Carrie to see herself as successful was to show her that her authentic self was already reflected in her business, and that she had created a business based on what was true to her. Her brand demonstrated her values, and her values were driving the busi-ness.

The point of this chapter is to show you there is a way forward. Other women have been where you are, and they have used the power of personal branding to discover their authentic selves and to achieve their business goals. Whether we're talking about Oprah, AOC, or our friend Carrie, it has been and can be done. And YOU can do it, too. Use these lessons from female power brands as examples of what to do and what *not* to do.

POWER UP...

We are going to use the women power brands in your life as inspiration to propel you forward to doing the diligent work of building your own brand.

Exercise #1:

Make a list in your brand journal of all the women in your life whose strength and power you have personally witnessed. They can be friends, family, celebrities, authors, journalists, teachers, etc. Think about specific, peak moments where they showed their power and strength, shining bright for all to see, or even too quietly to be noticed by more than just a few. Capture as many of these moments from these strong women as you can. Then say each of their names and express your gratitude to them.

Next, examine these peak moments. What happened? How did it appear they felt? What factors were at play around them that may have contributed to their success? Did other people prop them up? Did they get to the end of their proverbial rope and pull themselves up with sheer grit? What happened that you can learn from, to tap into and have your own peak moments?

We alluded to this earlier, this idea of examining what went right. It's a key theme in positive psychology – the science of strengths that enable people to thrive. The idea is, that by looking at what happens when people excel, e.g., professional athletes, high-stakes traders, business decision makers, etc. – we can learn about the qualities that propel them toward success and model the behaviors and conditions that got them there, to have our own successes.

Positive psychology also has a lot to teach us about the characteristics of high-performing people – from moms who multitask to teenage chess prodigies – and everyone at levels in between. We encourage you to read more about this relatively new branch of psychology in your pursuit of personal and professional fulfillment.

Back to your journal. This is about the qualities you admire in other women. You might come up with things like self-confidence, grit, determination, intelligence. When you're finished brain-purging on this, take a hard look at the qualities you admire in other women, and those you yourself possess. We'll bet there is overlap. And that you don't always give yourself credit for these qualities. Jot them down, reflect on why you don't always recognize them in yourself, and think about how you can coach your inner self when she needs encouragement.

Exercise #2:

Choose one of these women and ask if you can interview her. Take some time to make this an *event*: set up a nice lunch, coffee or cocktail meeting, and set aside at least an hour to be together. Ask her to tell you her story. Let her take this wherever she chooses to go: don't lead her. She'll tell you what is important to her, and as her story unfolds, you may be surprised to discover something new – about her, and about yourself.

Document her story in your journal *using her own words*. Pay attention to the words she uses, the emotions she expresses –

how she describes her peak moments. Document all the details, big and small.

Think about how you can learn from her. Remember to express your gratitude for this meeting, and for her presence in your life. We love that *"Empowered women empower women"* – so make sure you really savor the opportunity to talk to her, and to appreciate how what she is doing can help you.

Then Power Up! - because it's on to examining personality and the role it plays in your brand, next.

****

CHAPTER 4
Unlocking Your Feminine Superpowers

"Personality is the glitter that sends your little gleam across the footlights and the orchestra pit into that big black space where the audience is."
— Mae West

"Women are like teabags. We don't know our true strength until we are in hot water."
— Eleanor Roosevelt

As women, we have somehow been led to believe that we must travel to some far away distant land, or beg and plead with someone else to find our power. But here's the real deal – your power is already within you, and activating it is an inside job. It's at the core of who you are. Think about it, only women were given the awesome task of growing a human life inside our bodies and then bringing that life into the world.

If you are a mother, you know this journey well. Holding space for life as it develops in the womb, then birthing it when gestation is complete is a woman's sacred and miraculous ability. Our client, Debra Graugnard, Founder of Joyfully Living, affirms this when she says there are many *divine secrets* of this aspect of the woman. So, if you have the power to bring a new life into the world, you can *surely* conquer a financial spreadsheet, or turn the tide of a meeting in your direction, or learn how to promote your brand expertly.

Activating your brand power requires learning how to tap into the core elements of your innate personality. We believe every woman is a power magnet and can use her feminine power every day to achieve what she wants.

Have you ever complimented or heard someone else compliment a new acquaintance with words like, *"Wow, this new person is really something special!* She inspires, encourages and uplifts everyone she meets. When you are in her presence, you feel wonderful!"? That is the magnetic power we all desire, yet many women think is reserved for only the beautiful. Nothing could be further from the truth! We all have the power of magnetism within us, but some of us simply don't know how to activate it. We want to help you with this, so we'll talk about a few ways you can tap into the power you already have inside of you next.

It's helpful to know your personality type

Knowing your personality "type" is a good starting point for understanding what makes you unique, so you can craft your brand in an authentic way. Personality type is based on core elements like how you prefer to do things, how you prefer to perceive or experience the world, how you prefer to make decisions, how you prefer to go through life, and what you value. It is fairly stationary, changing in nuanced ways only, over time. So, starting with a good understanding of your personality type will help you as you flesh out the key building blocks of your brand.

There are several good, free, online assessments you can take (detailed in the Power Up! section at the end of this chapter) to find out your personality type. Perhaps the most well-established, and often used as the basis for spin-off tests, is the Myers

Briggs Type Indicator (MBTI). This is the assessment that provides a 4-letter code for your personality. For example, Faith is an INFP (Introverted, iNtuitive, Feeling, Perceiving). INFPs have a strong dedication to those they value, but conversely, one of their blind spots is a tendency to overlook their own wants and needs. With a laser focus on serving others, it's easy to lose sight of yourself.

Stacy, similarly, is an ENFJ, suggesting leanings toward Extraversion and Judging as the key differences between our two personalities. ENFJs tend to be idealistic and empathetic in dealing with others, and take personal responsibility for making the world a better place. But, they become frustrated when others don't have the same priorities, and are easily overwhelmed with negative emotion.

You may have noticed the common "F" we share. This is for "feeling" as opposed to "thinking" and is a core element of many women's personalities. "F" indicates that we tend to be more focused on feeling versus thinking – and that we are focused on people, versus things. Men, on the other hand, tend to lean toward "T" on this dimension...thinking and things. So, while women *feel* about people, men *think* about things. Makes sense, right?

There is a lot of science you can read up on relative to the "F" dimension, but one implication is clear: women are good at tapping into how other people feel, and this is a key superpower for us. By understanding where other people are coming from, we can determine how to best meet their needs. We can understand how to build bridges of communication with them. And we can help calm upset feelings.

This is a feminine superpower, and we're betting you can relate.

If you're a mom, think about how you and you alone can tune into your child when he or she had a fall or became upset about something. Mom's innate ability to quickly asses what's happened, how the child feels, and what the child needs, can be amazing. While your husband may be tempted to traumatize the child even more by immediately *first-aiding* him, you may be more apt to cuddle your child, express concern, and kiss his or her face before taking that next step.

As a leader, you may face a similar situation when someone on your team fails to perform, or makes a blunder in a meeting. You may be able to literally feel what that person feels, and innately know how to manage it. This is no small talent: with your feminine ability to understand others, you can manage them better, help them perform, and help your team operate more effectively.

This is just one example of how tapping into your personality can aid you in understanding yourself better and setting the groundwork for your powered-up brand.

BTW...big brands also have personalities.

Does this surprise you? After all, it's natural for people to have a personality, but a corporation? Really? The answer is a definitive YES. In fact, it's a *thing* in the marketing world, where we talk about brand personalities all the time. We often describe brands as if they are people, using words like "steady," "innovative," "popular," and "bold." This further clarifies and differentiates them from one another for marketing purposes, so when we're developing advertising, we can think about the brand as a person and ask questions like: What is the vibe that we should bring across with the imagery? What tone of voice, and what specific language should we use? If there is music in the ad, what kind of feelings should we strive to generate with it? All of these executional assets further differentiate the brand from others in its competitive set. A vital aspect of the brand, personality infuses it with life and creates an effective method of connecting to its customers and attracting new ones. Without a personality, a brand would just be a product and set of assets and belief statements.

Think about the brand personality of some of the brands you know. Can you identify differences among competitors in the same industry? Think about fast food: if they were people, how would McDonald's, Wendy's and In-N-Out differ? All three sell burgers...but in their TV ads, their Twitter feed, online, and in their stores, they show up very differently and you can see their unique personalities at play.

There is a lot of research on brand personality, and you can easily find lots of content online to deepen your understanding of how brands discover, formulate and leverage their personalities. One of our favorites, brand researcher Jennifer Aaker, identified five core dimensions of personality that are associated with brands: Sincerity, Excitement, Competence, Sophistication, and Ruggedness. She breaks these down even further into traits, giving us a rather lengthy list of brand characteristics. You can read all about her research online, and you can consider which areas dominate your personality and work on integrating them into your personal brand as you develop it.

Once you've identified one or several different ways of thinking about your personality, here is one theory from positive psychology that might help you deepen its impact on your business and life.

High-Quality Connections

One of the modules we love to teach is the concept of High-Quality Connections (HQCs). A theory developed by renowned psychologist Jane Dutton, a professor at the University of Michigan, it suggests that any encounter between human beings is either *positive* or *negative*. According to this theory, there is *no such thing as a neutral interaction* between people; therefore, any encounter we have with another person will skew toward either end of this spectrum. And whether the interaction is positive or negative, it impacts both people involved in a significant way.

For example, positive interactions light people up. They create energy and make space for better communication. People in positive interactions have productive conversations, can problem-solve effectively, and overall tend to enjoy their interactions. Positive interactions have physiological benefits too, lowering blood pressure and heart rate, and regulating blood flow.

Negative interactions have similarly distinct, yet negative effects: the people involved feel bad, angry, sad or mad. It's uncomfortable, and not conducive to working together. There may be yelling, shouting or sarcasm, and people may walk away, cry, or clam up, unable to articulate clearly. Blood pressure increases, heart rate spikes, and the face turns red.

Granted, these two examples are extremes, and the fact is that most of our daily interactions fall more into the middle of the spectrum. But think about this in the context of your daily interactions: when you short-circuit a conversation or accidentally bump into someone as you rush past them, it may feel innocuous, but in reality, you have transferred negative energy onto another person. Now, consider the flip side: you ask the Starbucks barista about her day or smile at a homeless person as you walk by. In each of these scenarios, most likely you and the other person both feel positive about the interaction. There is a whole body of research about the widespread effects HQCs have on people in business settings: they can affect everything from working dynamics between colleagues to brand loyalty.

These effects led Dutton to suggest that positive interactions are life-affirming: they create space for people to flourish, and contribute to good lives. Conversely, negative interactions are life-depleting – they take away from a good life, and do not lend themselves to flourishing. And just think about the effects of positive and negative interactions on our bodies and minds…it's easy to see how striving for positive interactions, or high quality connections, can lead us to optimal mental and physical well-being.

Imagine what can happen when you adopt this theory and apply it to your relationships and leadership position…not to mention the world. In your daily life, strive for one hundred percent High Quality Connections as you are building your personal brand.

POWER UP...

Go find your personality type. Here are a few options – choose what you like. If you have time, do them all, for different perspectives. If you can only do one or two, start at the top of this list.

The Meyers-Briggs Type Indicator (MBTI), based on principles of Jungian psychology, is a perennial favorite. You've most likely heard of this test, and or dabbled with it yourself in your Psych 101 course in college. But did you know the assessment was developed by a mother-daughter team, Isabel Myers and Katharine Cook Briggs, and that their vision was to help people reach their fullest potential, in order to encourage harmony in diverse groups? What's really cool about this is that this work begun way back in the 1920s. These women were pioneers in psychology, self-help and you could say, personal branding.

The MBTI sorts personalities into four categories, each with four dimensions. You may be familiar with INFJs, ENFPs? If you've taken this test in the past, take it again, as your results may vary slightly.

An adaptation of the Myers-Briggs, the **Robinson-Shur Type Indicator** can be found on Career Planner.com, and is a short 15-minute variation that will also give you four dimensions, similar to the MBTI.

Similarly, but with a fun twist, the **Keirsey Temperament Sorter** correlates to the 16 personality types in the MBTI, and builds on work originally explored by Hippocrates. It measures personality across four temperaments: artisan, guardian, idealist and rational. Its founder, David Keirsey divided these four temperaments intro two categories (roles), each with two types (role variants).

The **VIA Strengths Finder** is not a true personality test, but this assessment will help you understand your character and strengths from among 24 attributes the test measures. This test is important for anyone that follows the doctrine that bolstering your strengths is the shortest road to success, and that rather than focus on and trying to improve your weaknesses, you'll be more effective in life if you develop your strengths. Obviously, something that we believe deeply in. We recommend you do this in conjunction with one of the traditional personality assessment tests to give yourself a really well-rounded picture of the assets you can use for your personal brand. Again – it's free, and available online with a comprehensive guide that explains your results.

Once you've done one or more of these tests, with a better understanding of your personality and character strengths in mind, begin to think about how you can incorporate some of the principles we've talked about in this chapter. Think about how you can encourage your natural personality to shine, and how living in grace and harmony with it might facilitate deeper connections with others. Pay attention to how your personality affects others and how it can be useful, or not useful, in deepening your connections. Document some ideas in your journal.

Exercise #2:

Finally, remember the principles of High Quality Connections and strive for one-hundred-percent HQCs with everyone you interact with every day. Remember, you have the power to affirm life or deplete life from those you interact with each day. Be mindful of this in each interaction, no matter how small it may seem at the time.

After living HQC-positive for a week, journal your feelings about living this way and identify two- to-three positive outcomes from your efforts. As well, if you had any less-than-affirming interactions with people – look at these too, and learn from them. How could you have shifted your approach, your language, your mindset, etc.? Sometimes, it's as simple as taking a deep breath mid-interaction to increase oxygen flow to your brain, and let your mind re-group before speaking more. Eye contact, really trying to feel what the other person is feeling, and allowing yourself to be fully present will help, too.

****

Building Your Personal Brand

> *"It is not until you change your identity to match your life blueprint that you will understand why everything in the past never worked."*
> *– Shannon L. Alder*

> *"Tell the truth, but make the truth fascinating."*
> *– David Ogilvy*

In the previous section we set the stage for the tough, but rewarding work of building your brand. Hopefully by now you are feeling motivated to roll up your sleeves and dive into the fun part: we are going to uncover your brand and express it visually. In the following chapters, we'll share the fundamentals of the personal brand development program we teach and coach others on so that you can do it yourself. Warning: It will involve work. And self-reflection. And refinement. Your reward for following through? You'll have a Personal Brand Blueprint, made up of:

- Your Vision, Purpose, Values and Passions
- Your Brand Oath
- The Persona of Your Ideal Client

Instead of small, quick "here's how you start to power up" exercises, we're giving you full-fledged, really dig-in deep exercises - the same ones you'd do if you paid to attend our workshops. Prepare to work, because as the saying goes, "if it's worth doing, it's worth doing right!" Now, it's time to focus like a laser on building your personal brand.

Are you ready? Let's go!

♥

CHAPTER 5

The Fundamentals: Discovering Your VPs

"I always wanted to be someone. Now I realize I should have been more specific."

– Lily Tomlin

In this chapter, we are going to get specific about your brand. We are going to take you through a series of exercises that are very carefully chosen for their ability to focus you on the key building blocks of your brand. Just like Apple or Disney didn't just *make it up*, neither will you. You're going to spend a lot of time here really digging deep and being real with yourself.

The very first step in developing your personal brand is getting in touch with four key components of your brand. We look at them as the fundamentals: they are your Vision, Purpose, Values and Passions. Every brand is built on these four components; without them, you may have services and products, but nothing emotionally compelling upon which to promote them. With them, you still have services and products but now you also have a have a defined set of expectations about the ways you can deliver these things that are unique to you and that nobody else can offer. This makes a more emotional appeal to your prospective customers.

It's important to remember that *no other person* in the world has the exact same combination of these elements as you have. So, if you're similar to other competitors in your space in terms of what you offer, or what your Purpose is – once you put all these elements together, you'll have a unique proposition to offer the world. And then, when you layer on your personality…that's when the magic happens.

So back to Vision, Purpose, Values and Passions. These are referred to as your "VP"s - because they're a pretty big deal.

Your <u>vision</u> is brought to life by imagining your ideal world. The one in which you want to live, and you want to leave for your children, grandchildren and future generations.

Your <u>purpose</u> is your specific role in making that vision a reality. What are the specific actions you take or will take to help your vision come to reality?

Your <u>values</u> are the things you hold dear and believe in deeply. Many people value things like integrity, hard work, health, etc.

Your <u>passions</u> are the activities and hobbies that light you up, and that get you excited to do or to think about.

Having, knowing, and promoting all of these building blocks is crucial to a well-defined brand.

To illustrate the power of the VPs, let's look at some of the big corporate brands and how they are using them.

Tom's is a shoe company that donates one pair of shoes to a child in need for every pair they sell. They're a for-profit company, and though they make money, they believe deeply in giving some of that profit back to support causes they care about:

shoes for all, reducing gun violence, equality, and inclusion, to name a few. These are issues Tom's values - and they are not buried in their company story but are instead built into their business model, and displayed loudly and proudly for all to see. You can read about Tom's values in their advertising, on their website, and in communications the company sends directly to consumers. People choose to support Tom's or not, based on how they like the product, but also based on their alignment (or lack thereof) with Tom's values. Because Tom's is overt about what they believe in, it makes the decision easy for consumers: if you know their story and what they value, you can clearly say you're either a Tom's person or you're not.

From what we know about Tom's, we would guess that their *vision* for the world is one in which there is safety and security for all people, and the *purpose* they are committed to within this vision is helping people to achieve equality, fight prejudice, and lead fulfilling lives. We would identify some of their *values* as equality, security, and fairness. And, we can see they are *passionate* about helping people, sharing profits, and getting others on board to join them in these causes.

All of Tom's VPs work together to create a brand that is clear to consumers, and helps the company make decisions about where to spend their money, what to promote, how to create content, etc. The VPs are instrumental in guiding your brand to successful connections with your marketplace.

Let's take another brand example: Chick-fil-A. There's not a mom – or chicken lover - out there who doesn't know this brand's values well - they wear them very visibly in their restaurants and in their advertising and marketing materials. Family? Check. Supporting community? Check. Helping others? Check. Whether or not you agree with some of the nuances of their VPs, you cannot argue what this brand stands for. Their VPs are clear, and they follow the other two Cs of branding by being consistent and constant in what they believe.

So now that you have seen how they can guide your brand, let's get on to the business of developing *your* VPs.

It's important to know that you already have VPs. These are the very foundations of who you are – and they start to be formed when you are very young. They exist inside of you, though some are more visible or clearer than others. So when we talk about authenticity being a key component of branding – we're not kidding. It doesn't get more authentic than you as a kid.

But this is worthy of deep introspection, because certain elements of these components may have been clearer to you as a child than they are today, while others may have changed slightly over the years. Some may still be developing, though their seeds have already been planted.

Though your VPs are fairly stable as the core of your brand, they are nuanced, so they flex according to what is important to you at the time, your current goals and aspirations, and how tuned in you are to them. Because of that, we recommend documenting your VPs once a year to keep them current and fresh, so they can serve as constant inspiration for your brand.

To show how important re-visiting your VPs are, here's a recent anecdote for you. We were in a workshop and one of the attendees had gone through the VPs exercise with us very recently. I was afraid she'd be bored with the exercise so I asked to chat with her ahead of time, preparing to give her an alternative exercise to do instead. She told me she was really looking forward to the workshop and examining her VPs once again, because she had been writing some content for her blog that really excited her and she wanted to be really clear about how it connected to her purpose. Sometimes it works that way: you get a really great idea for a blog post, a whitepaper, or a speaking topic, and you want to make sure it'll reflect your brand well –

so you re-look at your VPs to make sure it all connects. Later in the day, she was psyched to have affirmed her purpose and connected the dots between it and her blog content, and she was feeling genuinely re-invigorated around her brand.

Our goal in this next series of exercises is to uncover your VPs. This is going to take time, as you make and refine each area, so allocate plenty of space in your journal. As with earlier exercises, we want to give you permission to be imperfect here. The goal is to keep going until you get each to a place where it feels 95% complete. If you can get to 100% - that's phenomenal! Many people tend to stop at *almost there*, with a reluctance to fully commit to 100% - and they continually refine the remaining 5% in each area...which is perfectly fine. These crucial elements are near and dear to your brand, and we encourage you to give them all the consideration and care they (and you) deserve.

Let's start out with #1 – a big, audacious area: Your Vision.

First, let's just take a pause and think about this. What is your IDEAL vision for the world? If you could create any kind of world at all, what kind of world would it be? What's the type of world you want your kids and grandkids to live in? What is the type of society you want to leave to the next generation?

When you imagine your ideal world: what kind of things do you see? How do people interact in this world? How does it feel to live here? In contrast, how does it feel in a not-so-ideal world?

You may want to sit quietly and think about this, or meditate, or daydream, before even opening your journal. Really try to envision what this world looks like...what it feels like to be there...who is there...and how your brand shows up in this ideal world.

Once you have a clear vision, open your journal and write about it.

Exercise #1:

Title this section "My Vision for the Ideal World."

There are a number of ways you can bring this world to life in your writing. First, you might write a story describing the world in detail. You could imagine yourself waking up in the morning in this world, and imagine how you might feel. Then envision what you see around you. What is the environment like? What is your house like? How do you do your morning routine? What do you do during the day?

Next, write some headlines you might find in a newspaper in this ideal world. What makes big news in this world? What is the level of dialogue people are having? Are they talking about subjects that are important to you? What movies are playing in theaters in this world: titles, subjects, categories? What kind of games will kids be playing? What kind of entertainment will we be binge-watching? What kind of music is popular? What's on the Bestseller list?

Thinking through all of these seemingly small details will help you get a good sense of what is important to you.

To help you get a better handle on how to think through your Vision, some of our previous workshop attendees have given us permission to share with you how they've addressed this area in their own VP development. Here are some of their examples, edited down once they were workshopped a bit:

"I envision a world where every kid has the same opportunities, and no one is more privileged than anyone else. People get ahead based on how motivated they are, and it's ok to say I want to stop here, where my priorities are. No one feels the need to out-perform each other, but we all respect what we each bring to the table."

"I envision a world in which people connect with each other, eager to find out about what makes each of us unique – individual differences

like skin color and gender and gender preference are seen as opportuni-
ties to learn, and differences are celebrated. People eagerly stop others
that don't look like them to ask questions and the people stopped are
more than happy to share stories. It's all about learning from and about
each other, in a true spirit of connecting as humans."

"I envision a world where everyone is secure, with enough nutri-
tious food to eat and access to medical care everyone can afford. So peo-
ple are both physically and mentally healthy and everyone has a high
degree of well-being. Food is really important in this world, so access to
food, safe growing conditions, family farmers and agriculture consult-
ants are all working together to help feed people and keep people men-
tally balanced. "

Go blue-sky with this. At this point, you are simply envisioning your ideal world, not yet thinking about your role within it,
how realistic it is to achieve, or what needs to happen for it to
become reality.

Also – if a couple different things come up for you here, it's
ok to write about them as two different visions. Eventually,
you'll have to choose a direction, but the other VPs you're about
to explore will help you understand which Vision to prioritize.

So, after some quiet reflection, get to writing!

******

Once you're satisfied that you've articulated your Vision in as
thorough and inspiring way as you want, move ahead to the next
element, #2 – Your Purpose.

Here, we are going to focus in on your role in the world you
just envisioned. Your Purpose is specific to you, and the things
you can do to help realize your ideal world. So ultimately, it will
link to your Vision.

Unlike your Vision for the world, which is more general, your Purpose is about you, very specifically. What have you come in to this world to do? Is it to teach, help, entertain, inspire, enlighten, educate, etc.? What motivates you? What do you love to spend your days doing, or if you're not already, how would you like to spend your days? How does your purpose lend itself to helping to create your ideal world?

When you understand your purpose, it provides a clear path to how your brand moves within the world. You are not scattered and confused, but lase focused on what you need to do. And, in return, your people are also clear not only on what you do but *why you are uniquely qualified* to do it, and how you align with what's important to them, and why they should work with you.

Shared Values

Now think about the role you have in making your vision for the world a reality. Let's start with an historical view: What have you already done that links back to your ideal world? Maybe you've already launched a business, wrote a book, or ran for office, in some way linking to your Vision. Looking further back, it could be a paper you wrote in grade school, a vision board you made in college, a talk you've given, a report you've written, etc. Anything you've done that is in any way related to what you can uniquely offer your Vision of the ideal world counts here.

Exercise #2:

Let's go back to your journal, and under the heading "My Purpose," write *Historical*:

List out and detail what you have already done that is related to your Vision. Really think through what you've done in the past and see where you can make connections. This is an important step, because typically for most people it illustrates that your Purpose is closer to you and has been more present throughout your life than you may have thought.

For instance, maybe you volunteered in a soup kitchen in high school or did mission work with your family as a child. Include all of these experiences if they seem at all related – as you do this exercise, connections will become clearer. We have had people in our workshops discover that they actually started living their Purpose as very young children – and go on to have wonderful stories to illustrate their commitment as a result of doing this exercise.

Of course if you've already done this work or something similar, your Purpose may already be clear to you. If so, that's great! But even so, take the important step of documenting it in your brand journal so all the component parts of your personal brand are in one place. And even if you have identified your Purpose already, linking it back to your Vision of the ideal world can be really illuminating. We do these exercises in this particular order for a reason, so just follow the plan and trust the process.

Pro Tip: *Keep extra space on this page, because as you start to uncover elements of your brand you will undoubtedly think of other things you've already done that now you can recognize as linking to your Vision and Purpose. Continue to document them to inspire your confidence.*

Next, write *Future:*

Here you are going to do a projective exercise to help flesh out some goals for yourself. This will help you understand your path more clearly, that is – what you want to accomplish in the service of your Vision.

Remember that exercise we did in Chapter 2, when we had you write your Obituary? This is similar, but with a less macabre slant. This time, you're going to write a news story you'd see 10 years in the future. It'll be all about you, and what you accomplished to help make your Vision a reality. If you can't get into an ambitious enough mindset with this, think 20 years into the future.

To facilitate your thinking, the story can be about you personally, about you as a leader of your company, or about you as CEO of a new company yet to be founded. The idea is to really think this through with idealism in mind, and come up with some good fodder for your Purpose.

Again, previous workshop participants have graciously agreed to let us share some of their revelations with you, in hopes they might be inspiring. Here are a few:

"New app launches that finds available medical professionals and matches them up to patients with limited money to receive high-quality medical care. Katie X. is lauded as genius and awarded Albert Schweitzer Prize for Humanitarianism. Said X in an interview, her entire life was getting ready for a moment like this, and she is gratified to bring medical help to millions of people worldwide. She projects being able to save thousands of lives a year with this app when rolled out globally."

"History was made today as 2030 marks the first year no children were killed by guns in the history of the US. Becky F.'s work with moms and kids across the country has been credited as paving the way for this monumental accomplishment. X started her powerful work with kids as catalysts for standing up to politicians and saying they were no longer willing to take risks just to go to school."

"More people report feelings of well-being than depression in exciting new research – Mia P. is credited for writing a bestselling book that offered a powerful program to help identify every day, easy things people can do to connect their diet to their mental health."

"Local community celebrates Monica H., a woman who advocated for more green spaces and contributed her design skills to beautify

neighborhoods around the city. Now, a new community center is being built in her name, and the center will offer educational programs to people of all income levels to ensure everyone has access to resources to promote green space."

These may sound pretty audacious to you, but remember, your Purpose is what you are here to do, and what you'll be remembered for. If you care enough to read a book like this, you're probably the kind of person who cares about leaving a legacy. So, why not dream big here? One thing is certain: if you set a vision and try, you may get halfway to your goal – and that can still be pretty impactful. If you never set a vision, you'll just sit still.

Have fun with this! You never know what is possible until you start to dream.

*****

Next, we are going to talk about the remaining elements, which are a bit like the *special sauce* of your brand: Your Values and your Passions. These elements augment your Vision and Purpose, surrounding them with more life, more color, and more dimension. And, they provide you with more ways to connect with customers and potential customers, by making you more interesting.

But unlike your Vision and Purpose, which are fairly singular in their focus, these elements will tend to produce fairly long lists – because let's face it, if you only have one Passion, or believe in one Value, you'd be pretty boring. So we're going to let you loose to think of a lot of Values and a lot of Passions, and we'll worry about skinnying down the lists later.

Like your Vision and Purpose, your Values and Passions have always existed, but because there are more of them, there is more room for nuance. So, list these out in rapid-fire, writing down everything that comes to mind.

Let's start with #3, and the second V - Values – The guiding principles of your life, your Values include the advice you live by and the issues and causes that are important to you. They are the deeply held convictions you will not violate for any amount of money - and may include things like honesty, integrity, faith, etc. Your Values are vital to your brand and do not change regardless of the work you do or where you live. They should complement and advance your Purpose and Vision.

These beliefs are so firm, you should be able to easily make a list of them. Think about the principles that guide how you live your life, the ones that are so important to you that if you ever violated them, you'd be devastated. We'll share some examples from others below to help jumpstart your thinking here.

Be as honest as possible because your Values will determine how your brand shows up to other people. And since they will help people decide if they want to do business with you, you must be forthright about them in order for them to come across as authentic.

So while you'll start with a long list, eventually you'll want to pare this down so you can effectively message your Values in a meaningful way in the service of your personal brand. What's an effective end number of Values to have? We aim for four to six. Too many values can confuse your messaging to others, while too few does not give you much to work with and promote to others. Four- to- six is a manageable number to illuminate who you are, while enabling you to remain focused.

Exercise #3:

Start your list in your journal, and remember, it's ok for this to be messy. You'll most likely start quickly but realize you need to refine your thinking halfway through. You're the only person that will see your journal, so don't worry about crossing things out or starting fresh on a new page. In fact, if you're getting into these exercises to that extent, you're doing it right.

So...start listing!

In addition to the examples given, some other Values we have heard people talk about in our workshops are:

- *Fairness*
- *Kindness*
- *Community*
- *Fun*
- *Growth*
- *Notoriety*
- *Honesty*

Once you have brain-dumped your entire list, go back through it and circle the 4-6 that resonate most deeply with you, and that you think will provide strong connections to those with whom you do, or want to do, business.

The, let's move on to the last VP.

*****

We are almost there! Just one more component of the foundational VPs. And, we saved the most fun for last. Now you get to think about and list out your Passions.

Component #4: Passions - Passions are the deep, burning inspirations that move you; pastimes, hobbies, activities you enjoy so much you'd sacrifice other things to do. Or, you enjoy so much and know so much about, you could write a book, or teach a class on it. These passions unquestioningly bring you pure joy. They are key to the way you express your brand, because they give it humanity and make you more interesting. That's why they should never hide in the shadows, but stand in the front row of your brand, loud and proud. Passions are great ways to connect to others.

When you are operating in one of your passion areas, you can easily get into flow. A flow state is one in which you lose yourself. Time seems to stand still. Do you know this feeling? Think about a time you were doing something you loved so much that you lost all track of time. Maybe you were shopping for clothes, and you ended up losing track of time and they closed down the mall on you (true story). Maybe you were throwing pottery and before you knew it you were late to pick up your husband. Or you were at the gym for what you thought was an hour but actually turned out to be three!

Positive psychologist Mihály Csíkszentmihályi (pronounced cheek-sent-me-high) – first discovered the flow state, and defined it as an optimal state of consciousness where we feel our best and perform our best. So think about this: what we absolutely love to do, can also lead us to high performance - and that can mean profitability for our businesses!

Your Passions are a great asset to your brand, for many reasons. For one, they can help start conversations and establish common ground with other people who might share your passion or at least be interested in hearing you talk about it. This is a truly great thing about Passions: when we talk about them, we tend to light up, become animated, and relaxed. This sets a great foundation for connecting with other people like clients, friends, colleagues, etc., because when we are lit up, we connect better with others. Isn't it more fun to talk to someone that is really excited about what they're saying? And isn't it great to have something you're really passionate to talk about with others?

Secondly, Passions give you rich fodder for your brand for content creation for websites, blogs, whitepapers, and speaking topics. It does require some creativity to connect Passions back to the other foundational elements of your brand, but with some thought you should be able to connect the dots from just about any Passion to your Purpose and Vision. So when you post an Instagram pic from your sailing trip (your Passion), you should be able to link the caption and hashtags back to your other VPs.

On this note, let's pause and talk about content. We like to advise leaders to develop content themes as part of their personal brands. This is a list of a few areas (3-4) in which you are expert, and can talk about at a moment's notice. Let's say your alma mater asks you to come talk to a class in two days: you won't have time to prepare a speech from scratch, but if you have some content themes ready to go, you should be able to whip together 30 minutes worth of content you can engage the students with. Content themes can come from any of the foundational elements of your brand, but they are typically derived most easily from your Passions.

Exercise #4:

So do this right now. In your journal, make a list of your Passions. Again, we'll start broadly and whittle down the list eventually. For maximum usability, we typically advise anywhere between 4-8 on your ending list. It's a lengthier list than Values, because they're *fun* ☺ - but don't let it get too big or again, it may become difficult for you to focus when focus is needed.

In past workshops where we've helped women focus on their Passions, we have seen examples like these mentioned:

- *Rock climbing*
- *Painting*
- *Reading*
- *Photography*

- *Running*
- *Pottery*
- *Writing poetry*
- *Antique hunting*
- *Gardening*
- *Traveling to Europe*
- *Making soap*
- *Pinterest boards*
- *Decorating a room*
- *Shopping*
- *Branding (ok, we threw that one in there from us…no one we've trained has actually said branding is a passion for them, though we like to think we've converted a few people to big fans!)*

Every item on your list should pass the Saturday-morning-sleep-in test, meaning if you have an opportunity to do it, but it requires getting out of bed at 4AM on Saturday after a long work week, you're still going for it. If something on your list doesn't pass the 4AM test, flag it and replace it with something that does.

Or try another vetting criteria: let's say you're at an uncomfortable/boring networking event and need something to break the ice: can you think of a way to weave your Passion into the conversation with a total stranger or someone you've only met causally? If it would be hard for you to talk about it, it's not a true Passion. Cross it out and find one that is.

Or maybe, just maybe, you can envision writing a book or teaching a class, or somehow otherwise gracing others with the knowledge you have in this area. If you have amassed enough knowledge, or you can see yourself spending months at the library and online researching the topic, it may be a Passion that qualifies for your list.

Once you have your list made, look at the connections between your Passions and your Vision, Purpose, and Values and start to think about how you can make connections that may not be immediately obvious. If you have a Passion that feels great to you but you struggle to find a connection to your other VPs...it may be worth keeping it on the list but flagging it as needing more exploration before it becomes an *official* part of your brand platform.

* * * * *

Congratulations, you've done it! You've gotten through an incredibly tough, but essential part of the personal branding process. This foundational work probably took you several sessions or days (or maybe one day with lots of coffee or wine), to get through effectively. You have identified the fundamentals of a strong brand and can now move on to two additional elements: your Brand Oath and your Ideal Client Persona, before we put it all together and create your Power Brand Blueprint.

So, let's go!

CHAPTER 6

Your Brand Oath – The Power Of Authenticity

"I had no idea that being your authentic self could make me as rich as I've become. If I had, I'd have done it a lot earlier."

– Oprah Winfrey

Your Brand Oath is a promise you'll make to yourself that will help you maintain consistency and stay true to yourself. It honors the work you've done to uncover your authentic personal brand, and will help you stay on track as you move forward with your brand. This chapter does have some workbook type work in it in which you'll write your oath, but it also rests firmly in psychology – a theme that re-surfaces often in the personal branding process. Specifically, we want to help you break old habits that can de-value your authentic self.

So…would you do us a favor, ladies? For your own sake and the sake of your sisters everywhere, promise yourself, here and now, that you will positively <u>not</u> compromise who you are and what you do. That includes:

- What you look like
- How you act

- The way you dress
- Your tone of voice
- What you post
- The people you socialize with
- The questions you ask
- The way you advocate for yourself at work, with your spouse and kids, etc.

Once you have looked within, examined your purpose and become clear on who you are (have you done the work in previous chapters?), there will simply be *no need* to compromise yourself in any way.

This is arduous for many women, but at some point, you will be tested, and you are going to have to take a leap of faith and declare, *"Even though this feels very bold and is slightly uncomfortable, NOT being true to myself is unacceptable."*

You can - and will - do this easily once you have firmly embraced your personal brand. Your personal brand will reveal not only the connection to your authentic self, but also some guardrails so you don't fall off and get hurt along the way. You will start looking at the choices you make a little differently, putting them through lenses like:

- Does this feel like the woman who has my VPs?
- Is this the woman who values X?
- Do I want to be known for X or Y?

 Granted, it's not always easy, but the biggest choices - the ones where you have the most to lose - are also the ones that offer the *biggest rewards*. The reason why you must be your authentic self is because when you are inauthentic, sooner or later someone will call you out. If you plan to "get by" simply by doing what others expect and feel comfortable with, at some point your strategy will fail. You know it, because you've probably felt it.

The question is not "have you ever heard of Imposter Syndrome" but "How relevant is Imposter Syndrome to your life?" How often has it held you back, stopped you from doing something you wanted to do, and are qualified to do, and from which others would benefit?

We've all been there, and it's not a fun place to be.

Let's dissect this phenomenon. Imposter Syndrome is that awful feeling where it seems like everyone must know you don't belong where you are, you aren't qualified to do what you're doing, and you just know you're not going to be able to hold it together for long. Imposter Syndrome is a mind trick, but like many mind tricks it actually has the power to change your behavior. Your mind tells you you're not ready to take on such a big project or so many direct reports, and it throws off your actual behavior. Before you know it you're messing up left and right and your mind is in the background saying "I told you so."

It's a vicious cycle, this self-doubt. And it's one that people who are sensible, humble, and practical tend to fall prey to. In other words – many women are plagued by Imposter Syndrome because we like to be prepared and if we are not, we feel it deeply. And that's ok – at times like this, we know what to do: we go back into our research, we get opinions from others, we put boots on the ground and we get to it.

But this isn't the only danger of Imposter Syndrome. The true danger is when we are already prepared, we are ready for the job at hand, and we still question ourselves. This is where we need to watch out, because this is what holds us back.

Imposter Syndrome is caused in part by not connecting with your authentic self, which should not be a problem for you after you've gotten in touch with your VPs in the previous chapter.

But, what good are your VPs unless you keep them at the forefront of your life, present in everything you do?

For this reason, we recommend writing an oath to yourself; a promise that you will stay true to your personal brand at all costs. That no matter how hard the going gets, you're committed to living life authentically. That you will see yourself as worthy and deserving of all the joy you desire, that you are valuable, and that what you do matters. To quote Emma Stone's character Abilene in The Help, *"You is kind, you is smart, you is important."* You'll keep this Oath visible throughout the day. Put it on your home screen, display it on your office wall, bedazzle a t-shirt with it.

A Brand Oaths is very personal, and can be written in the form of a sentence, a longer manifesto, or a letter to yourself. It is meant to motivate you to stay true to your brand, but it can also motivate a specific purpose as well, to be pulled out when you need it.

Here are some snippets from Brand Oath writing the women we've worked with have agreed to let us share to inspire you in your discovery process:

"Hey XXX, let's be real. You are an exceptional wedding planner! Everyone whose wedding you have planned has been blown away, and the reviews and testimonials you've gotten laud you for surpassing your clients' wildest dreams. You've made dozens of brides' and grooms' dreams come true on the most important day of their life. Your work will live on after you as seen in wedding albums from California to Maine. If there is a challenge, you can meet it head-on. You have the skills, ability and resources to knock it out of the park. Don't ever doubt yourself."

"I vow to be true to my Purpose so I can make my daughters and mom in heaven proud every day. I know my Vision is ambitious, but if I can move the needle just a little it will make the world a better place. Real food is worth fighting for, and I am one committed soldier in the

battle against processed and unreal food. I will educate others, and they in turn will talk to others. I'm in it to win it!"

"I'm going to be the next XXX Town Planner because there is no one better equipped to do this job. I've been in training my whole life to help people with the skills I've developed in school and in real life. If anyone questions that, I'm going to dig back into my personal brand and uncover 3 more examples of why I'm equipped to do the job. I'm not going to let anyone or anything throw me off my course. I was meant to do this."

POWER UP...

Now, write your Brand Oath to yourself. Try out a few versions until you find one you really love. You'll look at this each day, so you want to really love it.

You may have to take leaps of faith every day for a while as you read your Brand Oath and repeat it to yourself. Eventually, the leaps will get smaller, and you'll realize you are equipped to live your VPs honestly. They'll become second nature, and you won't need to repeat your Oath as often. But, it'll be there when you need it, like an old friend who knows you so well you need only to look at her to reaffirm who you are.

No imposters here!

CHAPTER 7

Aligning Brands: Your Ideal Client

> *"The secret of a happy marriage is finding the right person. You know they're right if you love to be with them all the time."*
>
> *– Julia Child*

> *"Finding a soulmate is an easy adventure, but the difficult part amidst the game is finding your kind of person."*
>
> *– Michael Bassey Johnson*

You could just as well replace the word "soulmate" with *client* in this Johnson quote. The point is, it's easy to find a client to hire you to do something for them. You can discount your services and offer a Groupon and have three clients by tomorrow. And these clients will likely be demanding, not well acquainted with what you do, and in the end, make you wish you hadn't made the offer.

So let us disabuse you of the notion that your ideal client is anyone with the means to pay you. No, it is not. Stop thinking that way. You don't need *clients*, you need the *right clients*.

Attracting clients who want to pay you the right price, to do the exact thing you're great at, in the timeframe you work best in...and who will talk about you to other clients, who will in turn also be a good fit for what you have to offer...these are the right ones, and this should be your goal.

These are your *ideal* people. The people who value what you do, and respect your time and effort while doing it. These are the people that will give you repeat business, buy new products and services from you, become valued colleagues in their own right. And sometimes, even friends. And in today's crazy world, who couldn't use more friends?

Attracting your people is something that requires a lot of thought. But you can't seek perfection unless you know what perfection looks like. So, in this chapter we'll offer some ideas on how to identify your ideal client, so you can recognize them when they show up.

Now, you may have heard us say that one of the key benefits of branding is that you don't have to hunt for your clients – they'll seek you out. Your brand will be so clear that it'll shine through in your marketing efforts, and be easily communicated via word-of-mouth, and people will just come to know your brand and what it stands for. This is true. But, you still should have an ideal client in mind so you can recognize them when they find you.

What is the bottom line? You must get clear on who you ideally want to buy your services and products. If you're not, you'll sell to anyone that offers you money, and you'll find yourself operating less than optimally while hating life – and that's the worst feeling ever.

So, let's focus on the all-important task of understanding how your ideal clients show up *in terms of their behavior*. In our years spent working at advertising agencies, it was not uncommon for them to fire clients who behaved badly. That's right: no matter how much these clients added a certain *je ne sais quoi* to the agency roster, good agency leadership could not and would not stand for unreasonable, combative behavior. If you want to build a powered-up brand, you must adopt the same practice.

Define what you *will* and *will not* accept in a client's behavior. Your standards may differ from someone else's because – much like beauty is in the eye of the beholder -- behavior tends to be subjective. For example, you might have complete distaste for clients who show up late or cancel appointments at the last minute, while another business-owner might abhor dealing with clients who complain about their fees and are always angling for a discount. In the end, every individual must draw the line between acceptable and unacceptable behavior for themselves. But, to paraphrase Yoda, *drawn it must be!* Trust us: it will be a game-changer for your brand.

As Meatloaf sings, *"I would do anything for love, but I won't do that."* We want you to develop that same resolve. To build and maintain a Powered-Up brand, you must set boundaries with your clients. Decide what your deal-breakers are, then declare them to yourself and the world.

Again, the definition of acceptable versus unacceptable behavior is different for each business owner. So you can't look to others to do this work. You, and only you, will set your desired client behaviors. There are however, a few basics we will offer up to get you started.

As a general rule, do not spend time and effort on people who are not worthy of your time and effort. This hurts you as a person *and* damages your brand. Remember, you *are* who you associate with. If you put yourself around people whose values do not align with yours, it will reflect on you in one way or another: others may start to think you share the same values and/or you may start to question your own values. Either way, it will detract from the progress you make in building your own brand. When you can say, "No, thank you," to an offer to work with someone who does not align with you, you know you are on the right track. Yes, it may hurt financially, but you will be rewarded with renewed self-respect and a calmness in your soul. And if we have gauged our audience correctly, our readers are not exactly wet behind the ears.

POWER UP...

To help you gain clarity on what this means for you and your brand, you are going to create two things: a profile of your ideal client, and a "Will Stand/Won't Fall For" worksheet.

Exercise #1:

The Ideal Client

First, envision your ideal client. What is this person like? Who is on their team? How do you feel when you're meeting with them? What kind of work do they commission you to do? How do they use the results of your work?

Create a profile of the ideal client, with substantial details here. If it's helpful, name the client. Marketers often create personas for the ideal customer and give this persona a name to bring him/her to life. For example, in work for a baby food company, we identified a mom who only fed organic foods to her little ones and preferred to make her own baby food when possible. To inspire the creative team to create advertising that really spoke to her, we named her "Jenny" and brought her to life through pictures and video. Everything from her clothing, the vehicle she was likely to drive, the food she chose, the crib bedding, and the toys her kids were likely to play with were part of her persona, and this gave the team a thorough picture of her life which then helped them reach out to her in their advertising.

When creating the persona of your ideal client, be idealistic, knowing you are reaching for the stars, hoping to get the treetops. In other words, you won't always get 100% of your list, but you'll be able to pick and choose what is important to you if it comes to it. And those items on your list that you don't get, will stand out as watch-outs for pitfalls in working with the client.

Exercise #2:

Guidelines

After you've created the ideal client persona, create a page for your guidelines. Here you will get very specific about behaviors you will and won't accept.

On the left, write "Good Behaviors," – and list all the things you want to see from your ideal clients. They could be things like:

- Treats me with respect
- Values my work
- Happily pays my fees

On the right are your "Deal Breakers," – potentially things like:

- Won't pay 50% upfront
- Negotiates aggressively about my rates
- Cancels meetings last-minute

Now, with this in hand, you have the building blocks for your Power Brand Blueprint.

Let's put it all together in the next chapter.

CHAPTER 8

Bring It Together: Your Power Brand Blueprint

*"Every day we have more ways of communicating
the brand. There are more places you can meet a
brand, and the richness of the cocktail you put
together about what a brand stands for is getting
ever larger and more complex."*

– Shelly Lazarus, The CEOTV show, 2011

Shelly Lazarus is the former CEO and current Chairman Emeritus of the billion-dollar ad agency Ogilvy & Mather Worldwide. During her tenure, O&M worked with brands like American Express, Kodak, Motorola, IBM, Ford, Coca-Cola and DuPont. Lazarus is credited for shepherding the concept of 360 Degree Branding and what she said in 2011 is even truer today: brands, including yours, have more channels to connect with their customers and potential customers, and must be thinking about not only developing a clear message, but spreading it through different channels in a clear and consistent way.

We want your outreach with your brand to be organized and logical, and to start with its core foundation - your Power Brand

Blueprint. Using the building blocks we uncovered in the previous four chapters, you are going to create it now.

Your Power Brand Blueprint will look something like this:

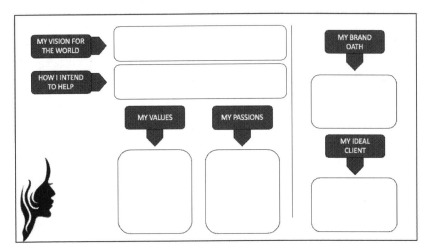

You want all these elements to come off the pages of your journal and onto this one piece of paper, one screen, one PPT slide – however you chose to do it that will make for easy display. You'll want to post this somewhere where you can see it often – near your desk, your bathroom mirror, your car. Some women, in the early days of working with their brand, screen grab it and use it as their desktop, so they'll constantly be faced with their brand.

We recommend you use an actual picture of yourself to personalize it even further. If you don't already have a headshot or branded portraits of yourself, get some!

Get used to this Power Brand Blueprint. Look at it every day. Talk to the woman whose brand you see reflected in it. Give her advice, inspiration, and a kick in the ass when needed. Power her up!

View this as a living, breathing creation. Change it when you feel the need. Infuse it with fresh energy when it feels stale. If you're into design, re-design it so it feels like your own. We've just provided a starting point.

And, at least once a year, or when you're bringing on new partners, changing jobs, or in any other significant transition, re-visit the entire platform. Repeat the exercises in this section from the beginning to give yourself a complete brand tune-up. And, if you're so moved, come to one of our branding events like Branding Over Lunch, Branding Over Brunch, and Branding After Dark – coming soon to a city near you – to share what you've done with other powered-up women who also have done the hard work of discovering their personal brands and love to talk about it.

*****

SECTION 3

Rock Your Personal Brand

*"Branding demands commitment; commitment to
continual reinvention; striking chords with people
to stir their emotions; and commitment to
imagination. It is easy to be cynical about such
things, much harder to be successful."*
– Sir Richard Branson

*"Personal branding is permission to
be yourself – your best self."*
– William Arruda, Personal Branding Guru

You've done the demanding work and you have your Power Brand Blueprint in hand. With that clarity top-of-mind, we'll focus on how to move forward with your brand. Remember the Three C's of branding? Now that you have Clarity, we're going to work on getting you Consistency. We will talk about your mindset, what you wear, how you communicate, what you spend your time and energy on, and the money you'll earn for the value you bring your clients.

The third C, Constancy, is about communicating your brand over and over and over again in places where it's bound to reach your people.

Are you ready to talk about Consistency? Let's go!

♥

CHAPTER 9

Power Mindset and Emotions

"It's time for us to have a voice. It's time for us to have power."

—Ellen DeGeneres

"To be outstanding, you must be willing to stand out."

— William Arruda, Personal Brand Guru

Women, it truly is our time! It's time for us to *activate* our power, which, for many, lies dormant deep in the recesses of our souls. It just needs to be activated. How do you activate that power? You have a great start now, by knowing yourself more authentically, and in having a tangible Power Brand Blueprint. But let's take it a step further and identify and activate your *power emotions*.

Women, a reminder: we already have the power, and we are not here to get anyone's permission to use it, keep it and flaunt it. For most, the challenge is figuring out how to activate that power without the fear and doubt that arises from others perceiving them as "too powerful." Well, we're here to tell you, get comfortable with it. Become accustomed to the stares and disapproving looks that say "Who does she think she is?" - that you may experience, or perceive to experience, when you show up fully as your authentic self. And prepare to shake it off, secure in the knowledge that you deserve to be here. You have every much a right to this place as anyone else does.

It's all good...your power will look amazing on you!

When most people think of women and emotions, there's almost always a negative connotation. *"Don't get so emotional,"* or *"You're so emotional,"* or *"You get too emotional."* As if emotions are a bad thing!

Any way you slice it, the concept of a woman standing strong and willfully activating her emotions is associated with negativity. We are here to change that conversation!

Emotions are good, especially when we activate our *power* emotions. Power emotions help to elevate us women to our full potential. They light up who we are as individuals, as women, as business owners, and as brands.

According to the Merriam-Webster Dictionary, the word "power" means to act or produce an effect. Think about a time when you took some sort of bold and noteworthy action. How did you feel? What was the result? Did you regret it or were you proud of it?

We almost always regret not doing something, but less often regret actually doing it.

We're going to share a story that - if you've met Faith, chances are you've heard before. But we repeat it here because it's a story that kicked off an entire career – a 20+ years in advertising leading to founding her own firm in which she's helped hundreds of women connect with their authentic selves and create successful brands type of career. So yes, it's important to repeat.

Faith's story: How I Boldly Powered Up My Way Into a Job at Ogilvy and Mather Worldwide

"I was enrolled in Hunter College in the communications program, having set my sights on becoming a news anchor. But then I realized quickly that you don't just start off in the number one major market in

the country; you first have to work your way up from the tiniest news markets – the kind of places I had no desire to live in - thus putting my news anchor quest on pause. Eventually, I decided to use my communications degree to pursue a career in advertising. I'd taken elective courses in television production and desktop publishing and realized this was now my jam: I was going to be an ad girl.

Ignoring the fact that the advertising business was an old white boys club, I pursued the dream that had been seeded in me. One day in the summer of 1994, I was walking on Madison Avenue when I bumped into one of my college mates, Annette, who was also working towards a communications degree. We stood on the corner of the east side of Madison Avenue chatting for a little bit, and she shared her exciting news: she had just secured an internship at Channel 47 Noticias. Being a Latina pursuing a communications degree, the opportunity perfectly aligned with who she was. No wonder she felt such exhilaration!

There was just one problem. She had previously committed to a seven-week gig at Thin Man Productions at Ogilvy & Mather, an opportunity she no longer wanted. My friend looked at me and asked, "Would you like to take it?" Well cue the power emotions! In an instant, they took over and caused me to act in a surprising way. Because without hesitation, I told Annette, "yes."

Meanwhile, I already had a full-time evening job with Mitsubishi textiles while still a college student. Furthermore, this gig at Ogilvy & Mather was only going to last for seven weeks, versus the full-time hours my Mitsubishi job offered, along with ongoing guaranteed pay. However, I just knew I had to get my foot in the door with Ogilvy & Mather, so I took the information from Annette and showed up at One Worldwide Plaza the following Monday morning. When I met the hiring manager, Donna, I introduced myself and informed her that Annette would not be coming, but I was here for the interview.

The power emotion of fearlessness emboldened me. At no point did I worry that this woman would think I was a total lunatic for showing up for a job that had been given to someone else – a woman who'd already completed the interview process. Here I was, boldly entrenched in my power emotions and showing up for myself. I had no fear. I did not shake when I introduced myself and my voice remained strong. On the other hand, Donna's jaw was on the ground!

She simply couldn't understand what was happening, but propped up by my power emotions, I felt certain that I was just where I needed to be at the time I needed to be there – and I felt confident that they would figure this out, too. Armed with that certainty, boldness, fearlessness, excitement and the sense of only looking forward – never backward – I got hired on the spot. Despite the hiring manager's initial skepticism and reticence, she offered me the job. I quit my full-time position at Mitsubishi for a seven-week stint at Ogilvy & Mather, and I just knew I was going to be a rock star once I got my heels in the door.

The seven weeks came and went, and guess what? At the end, they asked me to stay. I accepted a permanent position as a junior account executive at Ogilvy & Mather, one of the biggest, baddest global advertising agencies in the world. And I didn't waste any time powering up: my first client account was IBM."

We use this example to illustrate what can happen when you step into your power emotions – the ones that will always push you forward. Your power emotions won't allow you to question or second-guess yourself; they make you lose all fear. Your power emotions say, "Go for it!" Your power emotions encourage you, "Nothing ventured, nothing gained." Your power emotions tell you they're lucky to have you. Your power emotions communicate that you're a gift – fearfully and wonderfully made.

Your power emotions make them want you more.

5 Power Emotions

1. Boldness
2. Fearlessness

3. Certainty
4. Determinedness
5. Focus

POWER UP...

Say hello to your brand journal once again!

Here are two proven exercises that will move you into your power emotions.

Exercise #1:

First, we'll curate a PowerUp Collage:

Think about the emotions above, and any other emotions that you feel strongly are power emotions for you, and find some images that bring them to mind. Search online, look through magazines, or take your own. You can also incorporate the actual words, by writing or finding them and cutting and pasting them into your journal.

Make a collage of what you find, and call this your Power Page. Anytime you need inspiration, refer back to this page.

Leave a few blank pages after it, so over time, you can jot down stories about tapping into your power emotions. So just like all power brand women, you'll have your own power stories to tell to inspire yourself and others.

This exercise is meant to inspire you, so craft this collage well. Make it fun to look at, and use your creativity to give it your own personal flair. Think about the work you did up to this point, and use elements of your VPs to bring the collage alive.

Whenever you feel down, desperate or despondent, gaze at your power up collage to activate your power emotions. They are purposed and poised to get you back to 100%. Also – you can talk to us if you want a Done-for-you "I am Power" board.

Exercise #2:

Next, affirm your truth. To really help these power emotions sink deep into the wells of your soul and live there, we invite you to meditate on your power emotions. Whether or not you're in the practice of meditation, this exercise is simple and easy to do. Make it a part of your morning ritual – and if you don't have a morning ritual, now is a perfect time to implement one.

Close your eyes to connect deep to your soul while you repeat the power emotions with the words I am in front of them.

I am *bold*
I am *fearless*
I am *certain*
I am *determined*
I am *focused*

Repeat these "I am" statements for at least a minute every single day. To add real power, say them in the mirror.

This is a simple, yet powerful way to get powered up each morning. We encourage you to do this exercise with as much reflection and presence as you can; it's really a critical tool in powering up your brand.

****

CHAPTER 10

Power Presence – Dress the Way You Want to be Addressed

*"Because you are women, people will force their
thinking on you, their boundaries on you. They
will tell you how to dress, how to behave, who you
can meet and where you can go. Don't live in the
shadows of people's judgement. Make your own
choices in the light of your own wisdom." –
Amitabh Bachchan*

By now you probably understand that we believe everything about you, and every choice you make reflects your brand. From the car you drive, to the house you live in, to the job you do, to the way you dress, everything about you speaks volumes. #everythingaboutyouspeaks. These are all examples of the choices you've made, and they say something about what you value. This is true, even when you must sacrifice and make a less-than-ideal choice -- for example, you wanted a BMW but settled for a Honda – this choice says something about you.

In this chapter, we want to focus on your clothing, shoes and accessories...visible signs of your brand that communicate your essence – maybe even more than you know.

The choices you make with clothing reveal a lot about you. People will size you up in a hot minute, making assessments about your competence and values simply based on what they see. Though this doesn't tell the full story of you, first impressions matter. Of course, once you begin talking and expressing your thoughts and ideas, you'll have the chance to shift perceptions.

We want to help you make not only a good first impression, but the *right* one. In other words, we don't subscribe to the notion that there is one way to dress. Instead, we believe that your clothing, shoes and accessories should communicate your brand. This means, your Vision, Purpose, Values and Passions should all show up in what you wear, in order to communicate consistency. Remember the second C of branding?

So understand, "good" choices here carry no judgement or set expectation - everyone's brand is different, and we should all look different as we wear our brands with pride. We do not advocate standard, watered-down corporate dress. A sheath dress with a blazer over it may be regulation if you're an attorney, while bike shorts and a linen blazer is more appropriate if you're a creative. The important thing to understand is that the way you dress communicates *something,* and you want to make sure your choices are communicating your brand and what *you* want it to say about *you.*

"Dress the way you want to be addressed" is something our client Kristina Pernfors, CEO of Style & Aesthetics is fond of saying. We advocate that *you* always dress how you want to be seen versus how others think you should show up.

If you want to be known as a rebel or counter-culture brand, wearing pajama bottoms and going braless to a meeting may well accomplish your objective. It's about how you want to be seen and known.

If you want to be seen as someone who creatively solves space planning challenges by thinking outside the box, you should probably incorporate at least one unexpected item into your outfit.

This is the true power of freedom of expression. Our choices, when crafted deliberately, can communicate whatever we want them to. But we should always use clothing choices to communicate authentically who we are.

If wearing 5-inch heels to Publix is your authentic truth, then take that power walk through the produce section with great purpose and aplomb. Our client, Jacqueline Young Landi, CEO of JYL Image and Lifestyle, is the poster child for this. She will rock a silk gown and heels on a Tuesday, just because. She authentically owns her truth and has claimed the attribute "outlandish" as a signature of her style. She makes no apologies.

However, if rocking your Crocs in a pitch meeting makes you feel like yourself, then be that truth, unapologetically and consistently.

It's a fact that women tend to care about what others think – and we dislike being judged. Who does? It doesn't feel good at all. But we also have to realize that we're always being judged – this is out of our control. The thing that is in our control is what our brand says about us. So let's show them what we are all about, and take our power back.

Let's recall a situation that happened to Faith early in her career in her first job in advertising. A woman who was her direct report made a comment to one of her co-workers about Faith's appearance - something along the lines of *"Faith is very talented, but her look is too ethnic."*

That "too ethnic" look was a style called *Boxed Braids* that we also saw Susan L. Taylor, Editor-in-Chief of Essence Magazine and Bo Derek in the Movie 10 (minus the beads) wearing with great glamour and effect. In that moment, Faith had a choice to make: as the only black female in the department, should she cave to the pressure and remove the braids for a style more acceptable to her boss, do nothing, or double-down on her braids in true Power-Up mode? If you guessed that she doubled down on the braids you would be correct. Faith stood for the authenticity of who she was and her cultural right and freedom to wear her hair in the style that resonated with her.

"Stand for something or you'll fall for anything." That's what you must do at all costs. Otherwise - where does it stop? *"Don't wear those flared pants,"* or *"Carry a more conservative handbag."* It's the proverbial slippery slope women tend to go down when they don't realize that being told what to wear is stripping them of their power.

Remember the national crisis when our former First Lady, Michelle Obama, dared to rock her sleeveless dresses? Oh the shock and horror! Her toned, muscular arms did not fit neatly in the box of how "they" thought a First Lady should dress. But First Lady Obama does not suffer fools easily and went to defy conformity and set trends for women to powerfully and proudly show their guns.

Steve Jobs was famous for sporting the same black turtlenecks and jeans look while creating and innovating a whole industry. Gary Vaynerchuk rocks his knit caps and casual gear with pride and gumption and speaks on global stages commanding thousands of dollars. No one blinks an eye. And if they did, Steve and Gary V. wouldn't care. And that should hold true for all the powered-up women of the world.

Wear you! Do you! Be YOU!

POWER UP...

Here are a few things to think about as you consider your clothing, shoes and accessories.

Make sure to wait to do any of these exercises until after you have completed the VPs and have a working Power Brand Blueprint, because you'll need that clarity first.

Exercise #1:

We like Marie Kondo's "spark joy" method of assessing whether your wardrobe is in line with your true, ideal brand. For those of you unfamiliar, Marie Kondo is a professional organizer extraordinaire, and bestselling author of the book, *The Life-Changing Magic of Tidying Up*, who believes that every item in your life should spark joy. If you're following her method to weed out your wardrobe, you pick up a piece, assess whether you feel joy, and if you do, you keep it – if not, it gets donated or ditched.

This is an effective way of paring back your wardrobe and living more simply, which is also aligned with having a clear and authentic brand. Win-Win.

If you've Kondo-d your wardrobe recently, kudos to you! If not, set aside a day or to (works well over the weekend) to do this task. Our client, Marcella Scherer, CEO of Marcella Scherer Inc., an image and presence consultant for executive women, teaches her clients to "attack" their closets when auditing them – don't hesitate to rid yourself of items that don't serve you.

Be sure to donate any clothes and shoes and consider giving them to organizations that help women dress for success.

Exercise #2:

Another exercise to consider is building a collection of outfits that are consistent with your Power Brand Blueprint.

In your journal, dedicate a page to a few beautiful outfits you pull from magazines. Glue them in, and then write your key brand words and phrases that are expressed by these outfits next to them. You'll use this for inspiration as you take an inventory of your clothes, shoes, and accessories, holding each item up against this page and assessing whether it fits your brand. If it does, great – you can keep it. If it doesn't - toss it.

Really curating your closet can be liberating. And, remember to follow the same rules when bringing in new items as well: they must spark joy and reflect your brand in order to deserve a place in your closet!

CHAPTER 11

Power Language

"Language exerts hidden power, like a moon on the tides." – Rita Mae Brown

"The limits of my language mean the limits of my world." – Ludwig Wittgenstein

Power language helps you command a room. It makes people gasp, while it holds their attention and makes you, as the speaker, feel supremely confident in what you are saying. Power language clearly expresses your vision and helps to rally others behind it. It's the result of feeling confident about your message, being prepared to deliver it, and then sharing it with a powerful punch.

Power language is not just about choosing the right words. It encompasses your ability to command a room, not just as a speaker but a *presence*. Choosing the right words, emphasized by effective inflection and volume, distinguishes a powered-up brand from a basic brand. To be bold, brilliant, and unapologetically YOU, you must work at being powered up with your language.

So, what about you? When you speak, do people lean in and pay attention to what you are saying, or do they lose interest quickly? When talking to others, do you find yourself stumbling over your words, droning on and on, or walking away feeling like they didn't really "get" what you were saying? Worse yet, do you ever feel that you started a conversation with high hopes only to walk away deflated, feeling like you just let someone down...perhaps yourself?

Let's take the elements of power language one at a time and give you some guidelines for powering up your language.

Quantity does not equal quality

Power language is one of the few examples where less is more. The difference between a great speech and a good speech is fewer, more carefully chosen words. Great speakers tend to simplify what they're saying by using precisely the right words: when they speak, every word has a purpose. You may hear one of these folks speak and think, "Wow – why haven't *I* ever conveyed information that way?" It seems so easy, because they simplify to the point of elegance. They make their point with few words, punctuating them with power pauses to allow them to resonate before they continue to their next point. This type of speech gives you an ability to visualize what the orator describes, because you can clearly remember the key words and points.

Conversely, using too many words loses people. The brain doesn't know where to focus when presented with an abundance of information. Because it struggles to keep track, it tends to tune out. We've all been held hostage by boring speakers who complicate matters to the point where you don't know if it's you or them. I can assure you – if you're not fully engaged in a speech where you're leaning in and absorbing every word, it's not you – it's them.

Communicate with precision

One of the things we often need to remind our clients about is to be precise when communicating crucial information. A client, we'll call Tara approached her boss with some half-baked feedback about her team. She knew something wasn't right about the way a project was going, but she couldn't articulate the precise issue and how it made her feel (concerned, frustrated, let down), and the impact it would have to the business. Instead, she blurted something about the project not going well and being upset with her team. She used way more words than she needed to, and failed to communicate in a way that made her concerns clear. Her boss heard that she was concerned but didn't know how to help because he couldn't understand the issue. He told her, *"I need you to be precise when you talk to me,"* and sent her away. At first, she was upset, but eventually what happened sunk in, and she course-corrected and went on to address the issue effectively. We often share this story to remind our clients about the simple principle of using one's words well.

The key here is to really think things through before articulating what you want to say, especially if it involves critical feedback or distressing news. It pays to choose your words in a way that conveys you've put thought into them, and you are confident about everything you want to say. Every. Word. Matters.

Amass a great vocabulary

Choosing effective words is an art. But of course, you can't use the *right* words if you don't have *enough* words at your disposal. This is an excellent reason to augment your vocabulary and continue to expand it. You're never done learning new words and how to use them. Take heart: this doesn't have to be a big, onerous undertaking. You can expand your vocabulary by listening to or reading the news, tuning in to podcasts, looking up words you don't know and even incorporating non-English words to your speech. Sometimes the word that will most adequately capture what you are trying to say is outside your comfort zone, just waiting to be found. Your search for just the right words for your presentation, pitch, or sales meeting will be much easier if you have an abundance of words to choose from. It's a numbers game – so go expand your vocabulary and make sure when the time comes to choose your words you have a vast supply at hand.

Communicate with confidence

We can't write a chapter on power language without addressing one of the most typical things women do when communicating that undermines their power: suggesting we are unsure of ourselves by asking if we are being understood. I'm not talking about checking in with people by asking "Are you with me?" or "Are you following me?" – which is a natural and productive way of connecting, and a positive differentiator of the way women communicate. It signals that we care about our audience and want to make sure we are relating to them.

Instead, I am suggesting that the way in which we check in with others can either power up our brand or undermine it. Consider the following scenario:

Caroline is addressing her team and not getting a lot of visual feedback. She pauses to ask, "Does this make sense?" with a questioning tone in her voice that conveys she is not confident. Her team nods dutifully, as people are prone to do in a situation like this. But they leave with the perception that Caroline isn't one-hundred percent sure if she makes sense or not. Worse yet, Caroline goes away feeling like she sold herself out – because in her heart she knew what she was saying made sense.

The suggestion? Swap apologies for a true, authentic check in. You don't want to know if what you said makes sense, because you know it does. You're a bold, brilliant and unapologetic leader – why would you say something that doesn't make sense? What you truly want to confirm is whether your audience is getting it. But you can't ask, "Are you getting me?" without sounding like a jerk. Therefore, if your goal is to keep the audience engaged while checking in with empathy, a better question might be "Are there any questions about what I just said?" or, "Does this all track with what you are thinking?" to open the door even further for the audience to engage. These two questions communicate that you care about whether the audience is comprehending you, and that you want to open a dialogue if not. Furthermore, these questions suggest that you, as the speaker, have confidence in what you just said – confirming what everyone knows about your brand: you are bold, brilliant and in charge!

Give up weak words

Another issue women sometimes struggle with is using "weak words" – that is, words that undermine what we want to say by softening our tone; hence suggesting we are unsure of ourselves. Here are a couple of examples:

"Just" – as in, "I'm *just* checking in with you." No, you're not "just" checking in, you are checking in...and that is a beautiful thing.

"Wanted" – as in, "I *wanted* to check with you." Well, you are checking with them, so instead, say, "I am checking in with you."

Use unique women's tools: empathy and gratitude

One of the key differences between men and women is that women are highly tuned in to what others think and feel. Call it social intelligence, emotional intelligence – whatever -- but it is a key evolutionary instinct that has enabled women to care for their kids and maintain their community throughout history. In business, this tool's value is immeasurable because it gives us the ability to pick up on nuances that men do not always register.

Using empathy in one's speech can be powerful. What is one of your main goals when speaking to someone? It is to get the other person to understand your point of view. But once we achieve that goal, how often do we just move on, content with our "win" while think little of the other person? No, not every conversation needs to be a lovefest, but in our time-strapped and politically divided culture, we rarely express gratitude when we feel understood. While we may do this more easily in conversation with our spouse, parents, and kids, we tend to leave that out of key relationships in the workplace. But we shouldn't.

Expressing gratitude to someone – for listening, for engaging, and for understanding – can be a key differentiator in building a powerful brand.

Inflection

"I never said your idea was stupid." Have you ever done the exercise where you read this line, placing emphasis on a different word each time? Try it – it's amazing how the meaning and tone of the sentence changes as you simply change your inflection.

I never said your idea was stupid.
I *never* said your idea was stupid.
I never *said* your idea was stupid.
I never said *your* idea was stupid.
I never said your *idea* was stupid.
I never said your idea *was* stupid.
I never said your idea was *stupid.*

See? Inflection can be powerful.

The gift of the pause

So often in communicating with others we are in a race to the finish. In our hurry to get our point across, we rush through words. When the other person's speaking, instead of listening to them and taking it all in, we are already formulating what we want to say next. We miss entire points, along with opportunities to engage with others when we communicate in this way. Instead, give yourself the gift of the pause. Throughout a conversation, make sure that you pause frequently to take it all in: assess the other person's body language, facial expressions, and overall stance. Do they seem focused, calm, and engaged, or do they appear to be tuning out, frustrated, or overtly upset? Stopping to pause after you say something, or before you speak, is a gift you can give yourself and your conversation partner.

Exceptional speakers use pauses at the podium. Often, they'll have a glass of water and use it as a reason to stop, pause, and make sure their brain catches up to the emotional whirlwind speaking can be. You can do the same in conversation, whether it is with a glass of water; a deep, cleansing breath; or sustained eye contact with the person to whom you are speaking. The pause benefits everyone and helps to ensure your conversation is as heavy-hitting and powered-up as it can be.

POWER UP...

We want to help you access two vital elements: how you communicate when speaking and how you communicate when writing, so we've provided two different exercises.

Exercise #1:

For this first part, you'll need to record yourself giving a speech. You can choose a topic you normally speak about in front of a camera. One- to- two minutes will suffice. When finished, go through the recording and critique your words, noting the ones that reflect your brand and the ones that do not. Then, make a list of all the brand words you want to use and re-write the speech with them.

Exercise #2:

For the second part, print out a few recent emails, memos, reports – anything you've written recently. Go through them and with a green pen, circle the words and phrases that best reflect your brand. With a red pen, cross out words and phrases that do not.

Branding is deliberate. You want to incorporate your unique brand words into your speeches and writing as much as possible.

This is also an opportunity to practice both clarity and consistency for your brand. Clarity, in that your words can be a powerful way to ensure your message comes across exactly as you want it to come across. And consistently, no matter where those words show up – be it on your website, in a speech, report or blog – the same tonality is used, the same cadence, and the same attention to detail.

Words matter. Use your language deliberately.

CHAPTER 12

Get Focused: Do the Thing You Deeply Love and Master It

"My philosophy has always been, 'do what you love, and the money will follow'."

- Amy Weber

We live by that philosophy too. And we champion it with every fiber of our being to our clients. In fact, we have built it into our coaching program. To be precise, it's not just about doing the thing you love...for us it's about that deep, profound, I'll-get-up-at-4-a.m.-on-a-Saturday kind of passion. We have had the distinct pleasure of attracting some truly awesome women into our coaching practice who yearn to live that life and we are so grateful to be able to share some of their stories with you as a means of inspiring and encouraging you into your power and passion. The first step is always to get focused, which, we will confess, is often easier said than done.

As women, we perform multiple tasks because our feminine coding gives us power and potential. If you've picked up this book, you're probably the type of woman who regularly accomplishes more in a day than many people do in a week. We're talking about... make-dinner-while-listening-to-the-news-while-helping-the-kids-with-homework-while-flitting-back-and-forth-to-your-laptop-to-work-on-a-report-while-checking-emails-on-your-cell-phone-busy. We get you. That describes our nights too. But we need to realize that just because we can, doesn't mean we should.

Let's talk a bit about focus, and why it's important. Bestselling Author, Malcolm Gladwell put forth the "10,000-hour rule" a decade ago, suggesting that with enough practice anyone can reach the level of mastery and become an expert. A few years later, that rule was challenged by psychological research that counters it is not the number of hours you practice, but the focus you have while you practice that is important. What works for you may be somewhere in the middle, and that's ok.

The bottom line is a clear focus on a few things will lead to mastery, versus spreading oneself too thin, which leads to being just average in all areas.

One way to know if you are truly focusing is to determine if you are in flow. Remember? We talked about this awhile back (Chapter 5). As a refresher, a flow state is defined as one in which you are so focused, you lose track of time and other elements around you. Well here's something else about flow: we get in flow when we achieve the perfect combination of feeling challenged and feeling competent. In other words, we must feel challenged by what we are doing, but we must be able to rise to that challenge because our skills are up to it. A flow state feels euphoric; when in it you can accomplish more than you ever thought possible.

But we want to talk about focus and flow as it relates to your business. In this sense, it involves focusing on doing one thing exceptionally well to help your clients understand what you can do for them. And, we have a story to share that may help inspire you around this idea. It's about a client, named Dawn.

When we first met Dawn V. Gilmore, she introduced herself as a photographer who shot images of everything from babies to brides and everything in-between. She had been in business for nine years and was busy building that business with a host of strategies from ads to networking and anything else she could think of.

After attending the *Branding Over Brunch* and *Branding Over Lunch* events, she decided to enroll in our Real You Branding program to build her brand. One of the first things we noticed when she told us about her brand is the fact that she was doing too much! Shooting pictures of anyone and everything left her little time to get really good at any one thing. Though she had a successful business, she felt stressed all the time and wasn't finding a lot of fulfillment in her work.

Being a jill-of-all-trades is *never* a winning strategy. It feels desperate and lacks conviction - both of which are terrible in their own ways.

So working together, we explored what truly inspired her; what made her lose herself in flow, and what she felt most proud of over the course of her career. It turned out she loved photographing women and that she had a unique ability to bring out their feminine power and make it shine in photos. When we suggested she focus her brand on shooting only women, she immediately pushed back! She felt sure she would lose business with such a narrow focus. But because of her passion and the alignment this focus had with her Purpose to make women feel great about themselves, she agreed to try it.

After re-launching her brand as a Women's Empowerment Photographer, she had her highest grossing year without having to buy a single Facebook ad! Today, she is booked out solid months in advance and her name is well known among women up and down the east coast. If you ever see someone on Facebook ask for recommendations for a photographer to shoot women, it's almost guaranteed that Dawn's name will appear in the comments and her work will be tagged multiple times.

How does Dawn feel today?

"My business has exploded ever since I built my brand with Faith and Stacy. It was the best decision I have made. I have had the highest grossing year since I started my business 12 years ago."
— *Dawn V. Gilmore, Women's Empowerment Photographer*

We're super gratified to hear Dawn say it was the best decision she has ever made. Her brand is on fire!

And, it's only fitting that Dawn shot the cover photos for this book, which capture our personal brands so well.

Let's look to another one of our clients, Jill Lebofsky, known as the Midlife Mojo Master. Since Jill is a prolific writer, we decided it would be best if you heard directly from her about how narrowing her focus has transformed her brand and taken her to higher profits.

"In the Fall of 2018, I took a literal leap of faith in starting my personal branding journey and it was the best business decision I have made in a very long time. I really couldn't afford it and borrowed money and took on an outside, part-time job to make it work because I felt it was going to be worth every cent. And honestly, in the end, it was worth way more! Branding was exactly what I needed to take my business online and increase its visibility and recognition.

After doing the VPs and other key branding exercises, I launched my "Melt The Midlife Middle 28 Day Jumpstart Program," incorporating all the things I loved to do and on a topic I felt most passionate about. Following a branding program helped me to really pinpoint these things. I made more money on that launch than I had in the two years prior, and my business continues to grow each month. I also completed and published my second book. OMG! Branding helped me devise a way to not only sell more books but to bring new people into my community. Right before my branding journey I was depressed and lost in my business; now I am so excited for what lies ahead!"

We are so grateful to have Jill in our tribe, and to have been her guide and beacon as she powered up her brand!

So now that you have some evidence of the power of focus, this is a perfect time to focus your brand. Many women worry that by focusing on one thing, e.g., picking a major, you'll have to give up some minors that you love. The exercise below is designed to show you that you can, in fact, retain several passion areas while focusing your business and achieving better profitability. Read on to get in flow!

POWER UP...

If you have a business or if you're considering consulting:

- List out all the services or products you offer.
- Identify the one that you can deliver on the best, e.g., what do you continually get raves about, what do you feel you can do the most easily, what do you love to spend time doing? Make sure this is something your clients need that also makes money for you.
- Draw a pyramid and move this to the top. This is your "star" product.
- Underneath it put your other products. These are your "supporting actors."
- Use your star product as your north star in your marketing, when talking to new clients, and in social media.

Remember:

- Constantly increase your mastery of your star and supporting areas.
- Seek out networking groups, conferences, and speaking opportunities in these areas.
- Network with others who specialize in these areas to stay on top of trends and opportunities.

Focus, focus, never lose focus. Power up!

Postscript: Money Moves

"This goes out to all my girls
That's in the club rocking the latest
Who will buy it for themselves
And get more money later."

—Beyonce

Historically, women are under-compensated for the work we do, both in the workplace and as women business owners. In 2019, **women still earn** just 79 cents for every **dollar** men **make**. Pay-Scale's report indicated that **men** who own small **businesses** earn a **salary** that ranges from $42,575 to $96,111. **Women**, on the other hand, only earn $31,380 to $71,140 every year.

This complex problem has many factors at play in the background, many of which are not within our control, but systemic in nature. We'll leave the systemic factors to the economic experts working on these issues and focus on one of the factors we can discuss more knowledgeably: the psychology of valuing our worth and asking for money. This is really tough.

If you cringe a little reading about money, you are not alone. It is a fact that many women are uncomfortable with things like asking for a raise, setting rates, and valuing our companies for potential shareholders. We find discomfort in valuing our worth and in talking to others about it. But without an accurate assessment and pricing for our work, we tend to undervalue or even devalue what we do. And this can lead a business downhill quickly. If we are to claim our rightful positions in business, politics, and social leadership, and start earning what we are worth, so we can *get back as much as we give* - we need to fight like a man for our money.

So take a good, long, honest look at your pricing. Are your rates fair, to both you and your clients? Or are you short-changing yourself, like many women business owners and employees do? Is your hourly rate set too low? Do you tend to throw in additional hours without billing for them?

What about your time? Do you disregard the time it takes to travel to see a client, and only bill them for the hours you're meeting? If so, you're really short-changing yourself and you really need to think about what this is saying to yourself and others.

Sure, discounting happens and when it's in the service of building long-term customer relationships, or generating more revenue in future engagements, it can be a viable business strategy. If you feel ok about it, so do we.

But if you feel at all short-changed by anything you're doing, it's time to power up and make some money moves, today!

And here is where having a powered-up brand can help you. With a strong brand comes a solid understanding of your worth - and the confidence to claim it. Without a strong brand, it becomes easy to answer the question *"Why do I deserve to get paid as much - or more - than anyone else for the work I do?"* With a strong brand, you stand confidently in the knowledge that what you bring *is* unique, something your clients can't get anywhere else - and this is where the price for your work really starts to drive upward.

Let's go back to the Power Brand Blueprint you developed earlier. What does it say about you that is unique, something that others in your field or cannot say? What strong values are guiding your mission? What about all the expertise you've amassed?

And your unique life experiences that can help guide your clients to new insights and ways of looking at their challenges? Remember, these are the things that only <u>you</u> can bring to the table: a passion for your work, based on your legacy. A resilience based on being tested time and again. A talent you've worked hard to master. It's *this* uniqueness that you are asking your clients to pay for.

What you are *not* asking them to pay for:

- Fake / BS expertise
- Shoddy work history
- Half-assing it

Try an experiment. Review your Power Brand Blueprint, revisiting what makes your work unique and valuable, and then find an estimate or an invoice that's due. Whatever you've been charging for your services, increase it by 10%. If it's an existing or repeat client that is used to paying a certain amount, note that due to the cost of [materials] [labor] [xxx] increasing, you've increased your pricing accordingly. When you send it, point out the nominal increase and invite your client to call you if they have any questions. Chances are they won't. But if they do, hold firm and remind them the increase equals X amount of dollars to them and that it is necessary to cover increases in your expenses. If you're selling to a new client, you won't have this issue, so you can even try increasing your rate by 15-20% if you're feeling bold. Just start with one invoice to one client and see how it goes.

If you've been doing the work this book has encouraged you to do (yeah, lady!) - you'll be feeling good about the unique value you provide to clients and your price increase will feel more than justified. And like our girl Beyonce says, *"I work my 9 to 5, better cut my check."*

So, go claim your money!